ESPECIALLY FOR

_____

FROM

_____

DATE

_____

3-MINUTE PRAYERS FOR DADS

Lee Warren

BARBOUR
PUBLISHING

All scripture quotations, unless otherwise indicated, are taken from the HOLY BIBLE, NEW INTERNATIONAL VERSION®. NIV®. Copyright © 1973, 1978, 1984, 2011 by Biblica, Inc.™ Used by permission. All rights reserved worldwide.

Scripture quotations marked NLT are taken from the *Holy Bible*. New Living Translation copyright© 1996, 2004, 2015 by Tyndale House Foundation. Used by permission of Tyndale House Publishers, Inc. Carol Stream, Illinois 60188. All rights reserved.

Scripture quotations marked KJV are taken from the King James Version of the Bible.

Scripture quotations marked NKJV are taken from the New King James Version®. Copyright © 1982 by Thomas Nelson, Inc. Used by permission. All rights reserved.

Scripture quotations marked NASB are taken from the New American Standard Bible (NASB 1995), © 1960, 1962, 1963, 1968, 1971, 1972, 1973, 1975, 1977, 1995 by The Lockman Foundation. Used by permission.

Cover design: Greg Jackson, Thinkpen Design

Published by Barbour Publishing, Inc., 1810 Barbour Drive, Uhrichsville, Ohio 44683, www.barbourbooks.com

Our mission is to inspire the world with the life-changing message of the Bible.

Member of the
Evangelical Christian
Publishers Association

Printed in China.

INTRODUCTION

Got 3 minutes, Dad? . . .

You'll find just the wisdom you need in *3-Minute Prayers for Dads.*

This practical, encouraging book packs a powerful dose of inspiration into 3 short minutes.

- Minute 1: scripture to meditate on

- Minute 2: a just-right-sized devotional prayer

- Minute 3: a question for further reflection

Each day's prayer meets you right where you are and is a great way for you to begin or end your day. Read on. . .and be blessed!

FULLY MATURE IN CHRIST

He is the one we proclaim, admonishing and teaching everyone with all wisdom, so that we may present everyone fully mature in Christ.
Colossians 1:28

Father, when I read a verse like today's, I'm honored and humbled to know that it is my privilege and responsibility to proclaim Christ to my family, admonishing and teaching them in Your ways so all of us will stand before You one day fully mature in Christ. This is my passion, Lord. But it is also my burden because I'm a sinful man. Help me to stay the course, both in my personal life and in my role as a father and husband. And give me the wisdom to know when to admonish and when to encourage my family so we don't fall short.

THINK ABOUT IT:

What are you currently doing to make sure your family can be presented fully mature in Christ?

AN ACCURATE PORTRAYAL

Fathers, do not embitter your children,
or they will become discouraged.
COLOSSIANS 3:21

Father, I always pause when I reach this verse in Your Word, wondering if I have embittered my children in any way. Commentators say this means that I am not to be unreasonable with my commands, needlessly severe, or exhibiting much anger. I fear that I have violated all three at times, but that is not my heart. I earnestly desire to be tender with my children and to bring them up to be strong believers.

Forgive me where I've failed my children, and empower me to not fail them again. Give me Your nature—one that is compassionate and gracious, slow to anger, and abounding in love and faithfulness, as expressed in Psalm 86:15, so I can accurately portray You to them.

THINK ABOUT IT:

Twenty years from now, what will your children say about the spirit of your leadership when they were growing up? Will they say you were encouraging or that you made them resentful?

MAKE ME AN EPAPHRAS, LORD

Epaphras, who is one of you and a servant of Christ Jesus, sends greetings. He is always wrestling in prayer for you, that you may stand firm in all the will of God, mature and fully assured.
Colossians 4:12

Lord, just as Epaphras wrestled in prayer for his fellow parishioners in Colossae, I want to be a man who wrestles in prayer for my wife and children. Wrestling in prayer for them demonstrates that I know them so intimately that I know their hearts' desires as well as their struggles, and that allows me to bring both before the throne of grace on their behalf.

Forgive me for the areas in which I've fallen short in being fully engaged with my family to the point that I can pray such prayers. Change my heart, oh God. May my children's children look back one day and know me as an Epaphras.

THINK ABOUT IT:

Do you know what your wife and children are struggling with right now?

AMAZING GRACE

Then King David went in and sat before the LORD, and he said: "Who am I, LORD God, and what is my family, that you have brought me this far? And as if this were not enough in your sight, my God, you have spoken about the future of the house of your servant. You, LORD God, have looked on me as though I were the most exalted of men."
1 CHRONICLES 17:16–17

Knowing that John Newton was inspired by this verse to write "Amazing Grace" puts me in the proper mindset to ask the same question: *Who am I, Lord God, and what is my family, that You have brought me this far?* For I know many families who have sacrificed more and done more for Your kingdom. Yet You have been faithful to us. Thank You, God, for Your amazing grace. It's a grace we cannot grasp.

THINK ABOUT IT:

Who are you and what is your family, that the Lord brought you this far?

ENCOURAGE, COMFORT, URGE

For you know that we dealt with each of you as a father deals with his own children, encouraging, comforting and urging you to live lives worthy of God, who calls you into his kingdom and glory.
1 Thessalonians 2:11–12

In today's verses, the apostle Paul lays out three primary actions that a father takes in dealing with his children—to encourage, to comfort, and to urge them to live lives worthy of God. Am I strong in all three areas when it comes to my children, Lord? How could I improve? Send people and messages into my life to help me become the ultimate encourager, comforter, and urger, for I know of no higher calling than to point my children to Your kingdom, for Your glory.

THINK ABOUT IT:

If your children were asked to summarize your parenting, would they pinpoint these three characteristics? If not, how can you change that, beginning today?

LASTING HOPE

For what is our hope, our joy, or the crown in which we will glory in the presence of our Lord Jesus when he comes? Is it not you? Indeed, you are our glory and joy.
1 THESSALONIANS 2:19–20

Father, this world offers many different types of hope, and all of it is temporal—hope for success, hope for financial security, hope for a long life, hope for health, hope that our favorite teams will win championships, and so much more. While there's nothing inherently wrong with such hope, it doesn't revive the soul like You do. I'd be much better off placing all of my hope in You and then modeling that for my family. Help me to set my affections on You and Your kingdom this day.

THINK ABOUT IT:

Does your family see you place more hope in the temporal things of this world than in Jesus?

GOD'S WILL IS SANCTIFICATION

It is God's will that you should be sanctified: that you should avoid sexual immorality; that each of you should learn to control your own body in a way that is holy and honorable, not in passionate lust like the pagans, who do not know God.
1 Thessalonians 4:3–5

Opportunities to lust are everywhere, but it is Your will, Father, that I should learn to avoid sexual immorality, to control my sexual appetites so they can be fully expressed in the marriage bed. You make it clear in today's verses that such self-control is both possible and what You desire. Create in me a clean heart, oh God, and renew a steadfast spirit within me. May I only have eyes for my wife.

THINK ABOUT IT:

Are you too easy on yourself when it comes to lustful thoughts or lingering glances? What can you do to control them?

A QUIET LIFE

Make it your ambition to lead a quiet life: You should mind your own business and work with your hands, just as we told you, so that your daily life may win the respect of outsiders and so that you will not be dependent on anybody.
1 Thessalonians 4:11–12

The culture around me tells me the opposite of the message in these verses. It tells me to grab all I can, to point to my accomplishments, to climb the corporate ladder by any means possible. Meanwhile, Your Word says to lead a quiet life, to mind my own business, and to work with my hands; and in so doing, I will win the respect of outsiders. Give me that heart and that spirit, Lord. Help me decrease so You can increase.

THINK ABOUT IT:

What is your ambition? Are you quick to seek attention, or are you content to live a quiet life?

WARNING THE IDLE

*And we urge you, brothers and sisters,
warn those who are idle and disruptive,
encourage the disheartened, help the
weak, be patient with everyone.*
1 Thessalonians 5:14

Lord, I know the Christian life to be one of dependence—both on You and on fellow believers. Help me to convey that to my children. Help me to warn them when they are idle and disruptive, to encourage them when they are disheartened, to reach out to them when they are weak, and to be patient with them as they learn to crawl spiritually and then walk. And as they see me living out my faith, albeit imperfectly, may it point them to You and Your loving nature to help others.

THINK ABOUT IT:

The Bible calls us to be actively engaged in one another's lives so we can stay on the narrow path. Is that your natural inclination? If not, how can you overcome that?

FAMILY SANCTIFICATION

May God himself, the God of peace, sanctify you through and through. May your whole spirit, soul and body be kept blameless at the coming of our Lord Jesus Christ. The one who calls you is faithful, and he will do it.
1 Thessalonians 5:23–24

Father, I count it a privilege to intercede for my family. Just like Job prayed for his, and Paul prayed for the family of God, I do so this morning—asking You to sanctify my wife and children through and through. Keep them blameless, Father, as they go about their routines today. Make them shining lights in a dark world. I know that You are faithful and will do it. Thank You, Lord.

THINK ABOUT IT:

Do you spend more time in the mornings thinking about your work routine or the game you watched last night than praying for your family?

PASSING ON THE FAITH

So then, brothers and sisters, stand firm and hold fast to the teachings we passed on to you, whether by word of mouth or by letter.
2 Thessalonians 2:15

Just as Paul admonished the Thessalonian church to stand firm and hold fast to the teachings they had received from him by word of mouth or letter, I pray that my children would do the same with the instruction I've provided for them. Give me insight into which teachings they need to hear the most at just the right time, and make those truths ever present on my lips and in my lifestyle. Where I fall short, please fill in the gaps with supplemental teaching from pastors, teachers, and lay leaders so that my children far surpass me in the faith.

THINK ABOUT IT:

Have you considered passing on the Christian faith to your children in written form—maybe via letter or in a catechism format?

PUTTING OFF IDLENESS

We hear that some among you are idle
and disruptive. They are not busy; they
are busybodies. Such people we command
and urge in the Lord Jesus Christ to settle
down and earn the food they eat.
2 Thessalonians 3:11–12

The ease of American life sometimes leads to idleness and a sense of entitlement. But this is not the way You intend for us to live. Help me to convey this to my children as they grow up. As they begin to show proclivities toward one profession or another, give me the knowledge and wisdom to facilitate and fan that flame so they can settle down—putting off their childish ways—and earn their food as they get married and have their own children.

THINK ABOUT IT:

Are you making life so comfortable for your children that they might gravitate toward a life of idleness?

HOLDING TO DEEP TRUTHS

They [deacons] must keep hold of the deep truths of the faith with a clear conscience.
1 TIMOTHY 3:9

Father, I pray that my own family will hold to the deep truths of the faith with a clear conscience so we can be a light to the world and our neighbors. Help me to pass such truths along to my children, and help me to train them in the ways they should go. Help me to instill in them a Christian world-view—one that will sink down into their hearts and become part of who they are so that when they are old, they will not depart from it. May we be a people who continually ask: What does God's Word say about that?

THINK ABOUT IT:

What do you spend the most time talking about with your children? School? Sports? Technology? The gospel? Something else?

GODLY CONTENTMENT

But godliness with contentment is great gain.
For we brought nothing into the world, and we
can take nothing out of it. . . . Some people,
eager for money, have wandered from the faith
and pierced themselves with many griefs.
1 TIMOTHY 6:6–7, 10

Lord, I ask that You give my children contentment solely in You. May they never seek contentment in riches, fame, or pleasure. For all such things are fleeting and a cruel impostor. Finding contentment in any other place will lead them away from you, Father, as verse 10 suggests. It says that some who are eager for money have wandered from the faith and pierced themselves with many griefs. You want so much more for us, Father. I know the allure of this world. My family knows temptation as well. But may we never turn from You.

THINK ABOUT IT:

How are you modeling contentment to your family? Do they see you finding contentment in anything other than Christ?

EXPECT PERSECUTION

*You, however, know all about my teaching, my
way of life, my purpose, faith, patience, love,
endurance, persecutions, sufferings—what
kinds of things happened to me in Antioch,
Iconium and Lystra, the persecutions I endured.
Yet the Lord rescued me from all of them.
In fact, everyone who wants to live a godly
life in Christ Jesus will be persecuted.*
2 TIMOTHY 3:10–12

The American pursuit of abundance and security
is so far from what Paul and so many of the saints
of old espoused or expected. They expected
persecution as they lived out their faith in front
of a world that was incensed by such behavior
because it reminded them of their own sin. May
my family expect persecution, and when it does
come, may we rejoice for having been counted
worthy, like the apostles before the Sanhedrin
in Acts 5.

THINK ABOUT IT:

What sort of subtle messages do your beliefs
about abundance and godly protection send to
your children?

DAILY ENCOURAGEMENT

But encourage one another daily, as long as it is called "Today," so that none of you may be hardened by sin's deceitfulness.
HEBREWS 3:13

Father, I confess to sometimes allowing my schedule and my own daily concerns to divide my attention. I want to be the type of father who is remembered for encouraging his children every day to stay on the narrow path—one who is engaged in their routines and offering them gentle advice, while also encouraging them to think for themselves so they can avoid sin's deception. May I never be one of those fathers from bygone eras who checks out once he gets home from work, leaving my family's spiritual development solely to my wife.

THINK ABOUT IT:

What are your children's biggest concerns right now? How are you encouraging them through those situations with scriptural wisdom?

LEARNED OBEDIENCE

Son though he was, he learned
obedience from what he suffered.
HEBREWS 5:8

While I would never pursue it, I acknowledge that some of the best lessons I've learned have come in the pit of suffering. Father, I'm blown away by the notion that Jesus Himself learned obedience from suffering. Of course, He understood it, but He chose to learn it experientially. I shouldn't expect anything less for myself, my wife, or my children. With that said, continue to teach me through suffering, and give me the wisdom to know when to step in to help my family during trials and when to take a step back to allow You to do Your purifying work.

THINK ABOUT IT:

How have you learned obedience to God through suffering? Which trial brought you closer to walking in obedience to Him?

CHRIST LIVES TO PRAY

Therefore he [Jesus] is able to save completely those who come to God through him, because he always lives to intercede for them.
HEBREWS 7:25

When my children stumble and fall into sin, both now and in the future, may the truth of today's verse stick with them. Their salvation isn't dependent on their obedience to God, as much as obedience pleases God. It's based on Christ's finished work on the cross, through which He saves us completely. And, unbelievably, Christ Himself *lives* to pray for us. So not only did He do all the work, but He is also in constant contact with the Father on our behalf. May I imitate Christ as I live to pray for my own children.

THINK ABOUT IT:

What have you taught your children about their salvation? How does this verse affirm or confront that teaching? Do they know that Jesus is praying for them?

A BETTER COUNTRY

Instead, they were longing for a better country—a heavenly one. Therefore God is not ashamed to be called their God, for he has prepared a city for them.
HEBREWS 11:16

In this chapter of Hebrews, the saints of old were commended because they were willing to go where they were sent and do what they were told in faith, yet they still yearned for a better country—that is, heaven. Give my children the same yearning. Make them great citizens of our country—people who grow up to change the lives of those they come into contact with. But make them even better citizens of heaven—people who mature in the faith to the point that they long to praise Jesus day and night in the place He has prepared for them. And may they yearn for the day when their redemption will draw near.

THINK ABOUT IT:

Do you place a higher emphasis on your country than a better country (heaven)? How can you change your focus?

FOR THE SAKE OF CHRIST

By faith Moses, when he had grown up, refused to be known as the son of Pharaoh's daughter. He chose to be mistreated along with the people of God rather than to enjoy the fleeting pleasures of sin. He regarded disgrace for the sake of Christ as of greater value than the treasures of Egypt, because he was looking ahead to his reward.
HEBREWS 11:24–26

Help me to set the example in my family, Lord—to be willing to be mistreated along with the rest of the Church as the world scoffs at us, rather than joining the world in its fleeting pleasures of sin. May my family regard disgrace for the sake of Christ as a greater value than all the treasures of this world, for what is more precious than the blood Jesus shed for us to make us right with God?

THINK ABOUT IT:

What is your first instinct when the world scoffs at your faith? Is it to fight back?

CONSIDER HIM WHO ENDURED

Consider him who endured such opposition from sinners, so that you will not grow weary and lose heart. In your struggle against sin, you have not yet resisted to the point of shedding your blood.
HEBREWS 12:3–4

Sometimes my sin overwhelms me. Other times, it callouses me and makes me feel alienated from You, Lord. I struggle and fight and pray against my flesh, but I still fall short. Then I read passages like today's verses and I'm encouraged to keep up the good fight. I have never resisted the old self to the point of shedding my blood, the way Jesus did. May I be ever vigilant against the flesh so I can be the type of husband and father You called me to be.

THINK ABOUT IT:

What does your typical fight against sin look like? How long does it last? How quick are you to give in? Will you consider Him who endured even to the point of death on a cross?

EQUIP US, LORD

Now may the God of peace, who through the blood of the eternal covenant brought back from the dead our Lord Jesus, that great Shepherd of the sheep, equip you with everything good for doing his will, and may he work in us what is pleasing to him, through Jesus Christ, to whom be glory for ever and ever. Amen.
HEBREWS 13:20–21

Just as the writer of this epistle spoke a benediction, a prayer of divine protection, over this group of believers, I pray these same words over my family today. Now may the God of peace equip my family today with everything good for doing Your will. And may You work in us what is pleasing to You—so much so that the world would look at us and see Your resurrection power at work.

THINK ABOUT IT:

Are you in the habit of speaking benedictions for or over your family? How might doing so change your effectiveness for the kingdom?

A CHANCE TO GROW

Dear brothers and sisters, when troubles of any kind come your way, consider it an opportunity for great joy. For you know that when your faith is tested, your endurance has a chance to grow.
JAMES 1:2–3 NLT

Lord, help me to accept troubles as an opportunity for great joy and to see such instances as a chance to grow spiritually. I want to model this for my family and instill this in my children so they are not surprised when trouble comes. James 1:12 says that those who endure will receive the crown of life. That's our calling. To endure in the here and now for God's glory with the promise of the crown of life in the future.

THINK ABOUT IT:

How do you normally view trouble—as an opportunity for spiritual growth and great joy, or as something to be avoided at all costs?

WISDOM FROM ABOVE

But the wisdom from above is first pure, then peaceable, gentle, reasonable, full of mercy and good fruits, unwavering, without hypocrisy.
JAMES 3:17 NASB

Lord, wisdom is coming at me from every angle. Help me to filter worldly wisdom from heavenly wisdom through the parameters of this verse, both at home and at work. And help me to convey this to my family. I want to encourage them to read and listen to people who have more experience, but I want them to understand the difference.

Wisdom from above is pure. It's not self-seeking. It's peaceable, not quick to go to war. It's gentle, not forceful. It's reasonable, not unreasonable. It's full of mercy and good fruits, not vengeance and a spirit of unforgiveness. And it's unwavering, without hypocrisy, not driven by the latest trends.

THINK ABOUT IT:

Does the wisdom that you impart to your family match up with the characteristics of wisdom presented in today's verse?

RESIST THE DEVIL

Therefore submit to God. Resist the devil and he will flee from you. Draw near to God and He will draw near to you. Cleanse your hands, you sinners; and purify your hearts, you double-minded. Lament and mourn and weep!
JAMES 4:7–9 NKJV

Lord, give me a heart of repentance. Help me to never gloss over my sin or to treat it lightly, because I know that it grieves Your heart. And help me to model a heart of repentance to my family. When I err, may I be quick to ask for forgiveness. When I sin, may I be quick to repent. And may I be ever quick to resist the devil so I don't get caught up in patterns of sin. That's my heart, Lord—one that earnestly desires to stay clean and pure.

THINK ABOUT IT:

Do your wife and children know you to be a man of quick repentance? If not, are you willing to make a change today?

PATIENCE IN SUFFERING

For examples of patience in suffering, dear brothers and sisters, look at the prophets who spoke in the name of the Lord. We give great honor to those who endure under suffering. For instance, you know about Job, a man of great endurance. You can see how the Lord was kind to him at the end, for the Lord is full of tenderness and mercy.
JAMES 5:10–11 NLT

Lord, I know I'm not always patient in suffering. Help me to establish a routine with my family in which we will obey today's verses about looking to the prophets and saints of old to see how they endured. Maybe I could start reading biographies of Christian missionaries to my family, or I could play the audiobook versions in the car on family trips. I know You to be full of tenderness and mercy, Lord. May my family understand this too.

THINK ABOUT IT:

What can you do to show your family examples of Christians who have suffered faithfully for the gospel?

AN INCORRUPTIBLE INHERITANCE

Blessed be the God and Father of our Lord Jesus Christ, who according to His abundant mercy has begotten us again to a living hope through the resurrection of Jesus Christ from the dead, to an inheritance incorruptible and undefiled and that does not fade away, reserved in heaven for you.
1 PETER 1:3–4 NKJV

Lord, I want to lead my family in such a fashion as to always live with the inheritance Peter describes in mind. I don't want my children to grow up believing that the accumulation of goods, or having the latest gadgets, is the goal of life. I want them to have little affinity for the things of this world while yearning for the next one. For only You can satisfy the longings of a Christian's heart.

THINK ABOUT IT:

Based on the amount of time and money your family spends, where do you place the most value—in the temporal or in the eternal?

PLEASING GOD

For God is pleased when, conscious of his will, you patiently endure unjust treatment. Of course, you get no credit for being patient if you are beaten for doing wrong. But if you suffer for doing good and endure it patiently, God is pleased with you.
1 PETER 2:19–20 NLT

Lord, so many who call on Your name falsely believe that Your followers aren't supposed to endure suffering, hardship, or injustice. But Your Word is plain. Not only will we suffer such things, but we are called to endure them patiently, and Your Word says You are pleased by such a response. We have been called to this because Christ suffered for us, leaving us an example (v. 21). Help me model this to my family. May we suffer admirably and without complaint.

THINK ABOUT IT:

Does your theology allow for suffering for the sake of the kingdom? What is your reaction to the notion that God is pleased when we endure suffering patiently?

BECOMING FAITHFUL STEWARDS

Each of you should use whatever gift you have received to serve others, as faithful stewards of God's grace in its various forms. If anyone speaks, they should do so as one who speaks the very words of God. If anyone serves, they should do so with the strength God provides, so that in all things God may be praised through Jesus Christ.
1 PETER 4:10–11

Lord, help me to recognize the way You've gifted my children so I can encourage them to use their gifts to help others and to glorify You. Every good and perfect gift comes from heaven. I don't want to be a hindrance to the work of the Spirit in their lives. I want to help them recognize it and then obey. And where I fall short in understanding their gifts, bring pastors, teachers, deacons, and fellow believers to fill in the gaps.

THINK ABOUT IT:

Are you quick to encourage your children to serve the Lord in the areas He's gifted them?

STAY ALERT

*Be alert and of sober mind. Your enemy
the devil prowls around like a roaring
lion looking for someone to devour.*
1 PETER 5:8

Peter's warning to not get complacent spiritually is an important one for my family. Too much is at stake. Lions don't typically roar when they are hunting, which might mean the devil is even more ferocious than a lion. I want my family to understand that the devil wants nothing more than to devour them—that he's watching as they make choices, whether they are good choices or bad, and he's ready to pounce the second they stray. Protect my family, Lord. Protect our home. May all of us stay vigilant and sober minded.

THINK ABOUT IT:

On a scale of one to ten, how often do you think about what Satan might be up to in your home? What can you do to improve that number?

DO THESE THINGS

For if you do these things [goodness, knowledge, self-control, perseverance, godliness, mutual affection, and love], you will never stumble, and you will receive a rich welcome into the eternal kingdom of our Lord and Savior Jesus Christ.
2 PETER 1:10–11

We manifest these qualities as the Spirit enables us, but they are always there for the taking, Lord. I want to exhibit these qualities in my home. Help me to stir up my family of do the same, as Peter did for the exiles to the dispersion (v. 13).

When life is difficult, our default setting is reactionary—self-serving, a lack of control, ungodliness, and often hate. But we, as a family, don't want to operate on default. We want to walk in the Spirit. May it be so, Lord.

THINK ABOUT IT:

What can you do to change the default setting in your family when life is difficult?

ABIDE IN CHRIST

Now, little children, abide in Him, so that when He appears, we may have confidence and not shrink away from Him in shame at His coming.
1 John 2:28 NASB

May we be a family that abides in Christ. May Your truths be the topic of conversation around our dinner table each night. May we speak Your truths to one another as we watch TV, go to movies and various family events, and meet with teachable moments—hard moments. May we always look to You, Jesus, so that when You return, we can have confidence and not shrink away from You in shame.

We know that our salvation doesn't depend on our works, but we also know that we will be judged for our works. May we never bring shame to Your name, Lord.

THINK ABOUT IT:

What does it mean to abide in Christ? What can you do to inspire that sort of living in your home?

STUMBLE-FREE

Now to Him who is able to keep you from stumbling, and to make you stand in the presence of His glory blameless with great joy, to the only God our Savior, through Jesus Christ our Lord, be glory, majesty, dominion and authority, before all time and now and forever. Amen.
JUDE 1:24–25 NASB

Lord, I want to convey this picture of a perfect Savior laying down His life for my family. For indeed, He is able to keep us from stumbling and to present us blameless to You. You've entrusted me with my family, and I count it as my highest calling to lead and guide them to You so that one day they will stand in Your presence completely blameless and with great joy.

THINK ABOUT IT:

What are you currently doing to make sure the truth of today's verses becomes a reality in your immediate family? How about your extended family?

THE VICTORIOUS

"All who are victorious will become pillars in the Temple of my God, and they will never have to leave it. And I will write on them the name of my God, and they will be citizens in the city of my God—the new Jerusalem that comes down from heaven from my God. And I will also write on them my new name."
REVELATION 3:12 NLT

Lord, I want my family to be spiritually victorious. I want them to become pillars in Your temple so they never have to leave it. Write Your name on them so they will be citizens of Your city. Nothing is more important to me—not my work, my hobbies, my passions, my personal legacy, or anything else. When I stray toward these far less worthy endeavors, steer me back to the narrow path so my family will follow.

THINK ABOUT IT:

After meeting your work obligations, what do you spend the most time doing? Do you need to make any adjustments?

HE SHALL REIGN

And the seventh angel sounded; and
there were great voices in heaven, saying,
The kingdoms of this world are become the
kingdoms of our Lord, and of his Christ;
and he shall reign for ever and ever.
REVELATION 11:15 KJV

When the pressures of this world seem over-whelming to me, help me live with this verse in mind. The kingdoms of this world are indeed on the way to becoming the kingdoms of our Lord, and He shall reign forever and ever.

When my wife or children struggle with pressures, may they be able to see Christ's kingdom at work in my heart. When we receive bad news, put it into perspective for us by helping us to dwell on Christ's eternal reign over sin and death. When we fret about the political climate in our country, remind us that Jesus is the King of kings.

THINK ABOUT IT:

Are you prone to despair as you look at the ravages of sin all around you? Look up. . .your redemption draws near.

COMPARABLE HELPERS

*And the L*ORD *God said, "It is not good that man should be alone; I will make him a helper comparable to him."*
GENESIS 2:18 NKJV

Lord, You've said that it is not good for man to be alone, so I'm praying today for the eventual spouses of my children—fellow believers who will grow up to elevate Christ in their marriage and family. As my children grow, I ask for You to give them a spirit of calm as they consider potential dating or courting relationships. Finding a comparable match isn't up to them. Ultimately, it's up to You, and I trust You to lead and guide them in the process. They will not make a bigger earthly decision, Father, and I leave it in Your hands.

THINK ABOUT IT:

How involved are you in talking to your kids about their dating life? If you've been hands-off, are you willing to begin offering godly advice?

WRESTLING WITH GOD

*And Jacob was left alone; and there wrestled
a man with him until the breaking of the day.*
GENESIS 32:24 KJV

We all face You alone, Lord. Just as Jacob faced the angel and wrestled with him all night, maybe fearing that Esau might exact his revenge when he finally saw his brother again, so we as Christians wrestle with You, sometimes all night, other times much longer. But Jacob prevailed—in the sense that he didn't give up.

Hosea 12:4 (KJV) says, "Yea, he had power over the angel, and prevailed: he wept, and made supplication unto him." In John Wesley's commentary, he notes that Jacob's "prayers and tears were his weapons. It was not only a corporal, but a spiritual wrestling by vigorous faith and holy desire."

May this be the case with my family.

THINK ABOUT IT:

When God allows some sort of opposition in your life, how quick are you to give up, rather than praying and weeping through the trial?

A SPIRITUAL LEGACY

*"On that day tell your son, 'I do this because of what the L*ORD *did for me when I came out of Egypt.' This observance will be for you like a sign on your hand and a reminder on your forehead that this law of the L*ORD *is to be on your lips. For the L*ORD *brought you out of Egypt with his mighty hand."*
EXODUS 13:8–9

Father, just as You wanted future generations of Israelites to remember Your rescuing work during the Passover by encouraging fathers to tell their sons why they celebrate that ceremony every year, I want to be a father who tells my children about the rescuing work You did in my generation—in my very heart. May this truth be on my lips continually so that my children tell their children about it.

THINK ABOUT IT:

Do you have a spiritual legacy from bygone eras? If not, why not start one now? If so, why not continue it?

YOUR FAMILY REPRESENTATIVE

"In this way, Aaron will carry the names of the tribes of Israel on the sacred chestpiece over his heart when he goes into the Holy Place. This will be a continual reminder that he represents the people when he comes before the LORD."
EXODUS 28:29 NLT

Father, just as Aaron carried the names of the tribes of Israel on his chestpiece over his heart when he met with You in the Holy of Holies, I do the same thing this very day with my family. As I enter Your presence, I bring their names to You. May I never take this privilege lightly, and may I never neglect it. Too much is at stake for me to do so.

THINK ABOUT IT:

Do you name the names of your family every time you enter into a time of extended prayer? If not, why not begin anew today?

TEND YOUR LAMP

*The L*ORD *said to Moses, "Command the Israelites to bring you clear oil of pressed olives for the light so that the lamps may be kept burning continually. Outside the curtain that shields the ark of the covenant law in the tent of meeting, Aaron is to tend the lamps before the L*ORD *from evening till morning, continually."*
LEVITICUS 24:1–3

The lamps outside the Tent of Meeting were to be kept burning at all times, so they had to be tended from evening till morning. This is a beautiful picture of the Christian life. May I tend the light that is inside me from evening until morning, perpetually. For I know that if my light goes out, I'll be ineffective as a father, husband, employee, church member, and member of society. May it never be so, Lord.

THINK ABOUT IT:

Are you as diligent about tending the spiritual lamp inside you as Aaron was in tending the lamps outside the curtain in the Tent of Meeting?

LEAD AND GUIDE US, LORD

Whenever the cloud was taken up from above the tabernacle, after that the children of Israel would journey; and in the place where the cloud settled, there the children of Israel would pitch their tents.
NUMBERS 9:17 NKJV

Lord, may I lead my family according to this principle. Wherever You lead us, we will take up our home and journey after You. And wherever You settle us, we will pitch our tent. We don't want to be caught up in chasing the things of this world. We don't want to spend our lives engaged in useless activities and in places where You don't want us.

Numbers 9:22 (NKJV) says, "Whether it was two days, a month, or a year that the cloud remained above the tabernacle, the children of Israel would remain encamped and not journey; but when it was taken up, they would journey."

May we adopt that attitude, Lord.

THINK ABOUT IT:

Is the Lord speaking to you currently, telling you to pick up your tent and move?

SPEAKING THE
RIGHT MESSAGE

Then King Balak demanded of Balaam, "What
have you done to me? I brought you to curse
my enemies. Instead, you have blessed them!"
But Balaam replied, "I will speak only the
message that the LORD puts in my mouth."
NUMBERS 23:11–12 NLT

Lord, just as King Balak demanded that Balaam
speak a curse on Israel and Balaam was unable to
because he was only willing to speak the words
You gave him, may that be the case with me in
my family. May they only hear me speak words
that are consistent with Your Word.

Numbers 24:13 (NLT) goes on to say, " 'Even
if Balak were to give me his palace filled with
silver and gold, I would be powerless to do
anything against the will of the LORD.' I told
you that I could say only what the LORD says!"

May I have that fortitude.

THINK ABOUT IT:

How quick are you to offer opinions to your
family without first considering what the Lord
says about the subject?

GOD'S MIGHTY HAND

*"When your son asks you in time to come,
saying, 'What is the meaning of the testimonies,
the statutes, and the judgments which the
LORD our God has commanded you?' then
you shall say to your son: 'We were slaves
of Pharaoh in Egypt, and the LORD brought
us out of Egypt with a mighty hand.' "*
DEUTERONOMY 6:20–21 NKJV

Lord, I want to plant truth deep inside the hearts
of my children by using hymns, prayer books,
creeds, and, of course, the scriptures so that
one day they would ask the meaning behind
such tools. This will give me the opportunity
to explain how I was once far from You but You
brought me up out of the yoke of slavery, so, out
of appreciation and dedication, I tend my soul
with these various tools, to God's glory.

THINK ABOUT IT:

How are you practicing your faith in front of your
family? Do they see you studying the scriptures,
singing hymns, or diving into prayer books?

WHAT DOES GOD REQUIRE?

And now, Israel, what doth the Lord thy
God require of thee, but to fear the Lord
thy God, to walk in all his ways, and to love
him, and to serve the Lord thy God with all
thy heart and with all thy soul, to keep the
commandments of the Lord, and his statutes,
which I command thee this day for thy good?
DEUTERONOMY 10:12–13 KJV

The Christian life isn't for the uncommitted or weak of heart. You call us to be fully devoted, to fear You, to walk in all Your ways, and to serve You with all our heart and soul as we keep Your commandments. Lord, I fall short of this mission every day, but my spirit yearns for full obedience. Make it so. Bring me closer to You. Change my heart, oh God. Conform me into Your image.

THINK ABOUT IT:

Who has been the most influential Christian in your life? How close was that person to exhibiting the characteristics in today's verses?

SHARE THE WORD

"So commit yourselves wholeheartedly to these words of mine. Tie them to your hands and wear them on your forehead as reminders. Teach them to your children. Talk about them when you are at home and when you are on the road, when you are going to bed and when you are getting up. Write them on the doorposts of your house and on your gates."
DEUTERONOMY 11:18–20 NLT

Lord, I want to commit myself and my family wholeheartedly to Your Word. Give me ways to tie Your words to my hands—maybe in the form of a scripture bracelet. Give me ways to write them on the doorposts—maybe in the form of scripture plaques. Prompt me to talk about Your words with my children while we are engaged in family activities, before they go to sleep each night, and after they wake up each morning.

THINK ABOUT IT:

What is one new way you can incorporate the Word of God into your life that will lead to discussion with your children?

A LOYALTY TEST

If a prophet, or one who foretells by dreams, appears among you and announces to you a sign or wonder, and if the sign or wonder spoken of takes place, and the prophet says, "Let us follow other gods" (gods you have not known) "and let us worship them," you must not listen to the words of that prophet or dreamer. The LORD your God is testing you to find out whether you love him with all your heart and with all your soul.

DEUTERONOMY 13:1–3

Give me strength and clarity of thought to endure Your test, Lord. May I never lead my family after other gods—whether they be the love of money, success, fame, or status. I know their allure because I've been tempted by all of them. But they are lies from the pit.

THINK ABOUT IT:

Have you ever considered the notion that the false gods you are tempted to follow are a test of your loyalty from God?

THE COVENANT

*"All of you—tribal leaders, elders, officers, all the men of Israel—are standing today in the presence of the L*ORD *your God. Your little ones and your wives are with you, as well as the foreigners living among you who chop your wood and carry your water. You are standing here today to enter into the covenant of the L*ORD *your God."*
DEUTERONOMY 29:10–12 NLT

As the spiritual head of my household, I earnestly desire that my family would live solely for You, and that by being devoted to You, we would receive spiritual protections in the form of Your covenant that the world can never touch. As Jesus said in Matthew 10:28 (NLT), "Don't be afraid of those who want to kill your body; they cannot touch your soul. Fear only God, who can destroy both soul and body in hell."

THINK ABOUT IT:

Does your family see you as the spiritual head of the home—as someone who will lead them into God's protective hand?

MAKING THE CALL

"Call them all together—men, women, children,
and the foreigners living in your towns—so
they may hear this Book of Instruction and
learn to fear the LORD your God and carefully
obey all the terms of these instructions.
Do this so that your children who have not
known these instructions will hear them and
will learn to fear the LORD your God."
DEUTERONOMY 31:12–13 NLT

Father, make me more intentional in drawing my family together for consistent devotional times that are centered on Your Word. Life is so busy that we even tend to eat on the go. But may we never neglect the careful reading and discussion of Your Word as a family. Give me insight into knowing which portions to read at the exact times my family needs to hear it. We want to be a family that fears You, Lord.

THINK ABOUT IT:

Do you call your family together on a regular basis so they may hear instruction from the Lord?

BUILDING MEMORIALS

That this may be a sign among you, that when your children ask their fathers in time to come, saying, What mean ye by these stones? Then ye shall answer them, That the waters of Jordan were cut off before the ark of the covenant of the LORD; when it passed over Jordan, the waters of Jordan were cut off: and these stones shall be for a memorial unto the children of Israel for ever.
JOSHUA 4:6–7 KJV

I want to put today's verses into practice, Lord. Give me ideas to create tangible memorials of Your faithfulness—memorials that will outlive me and will serve as reminders to my children of how You are there for each generation. Should I start a journal for each child? Or maybe shoot short videos on my phone and upload them somewhere so that my kids can see them someday?

THINK ABOUT IT:

Do your children know about the Lord's faithfulness in your family going back several generations? If not, how can you change that?

MARRYING IN THE FAITH

"For if you ever go back and cling to the rest of these nations, these which remain among you, and intermarry with them, so that you associate with them and they with you, know with certainty that the Lord *your God will not continue to drive these nations out from before you."*
Joshua 23:12–13 nasb

I lift up my children to You today, Lord, asking that they would marry strong Christians—people who will take them deeper in their walk with You, rather than pulling them away from You. Later in verse 13 (nasb), Joshua goes on to say that marrying the wrong people "will be a snare and a trap to you, and a whip on your sides and thorns in your eyes, until you perish from off this good land which the Lord your God has given you." May that never be the case with my children.

THINK ABOUT IT:

Are you explaining the importance of marrying a Christian to your children? Do they see the benefits?

THE GOSPEL BATON

*When all that generation had been gathered
to their fathers, another generation arose
after them who did not know the LORD nor
the work which He had done for Israel.
Then the children of Israel did evil in the
sight of the LORD, and served the Baals.*
JUDGES 2:10–11 NKJV

I don't want what happened in these verses
to be the legacy of this family, Lord. Passing
on the gospel baton to the next generation
ought to always be our highest priority. For
when one generation fails to do so, subsequent
generations are sure to do evil in Your sight as
they serve modern Baals. If my kids are not yet
believers, keep this message fresh in my mind
at all times as I bring them up in the faith. If
they are believers, may I be diligent in encouraging them to remember to pass it on to their
children someday.

THINK ABOUT IT:

What are you doing to make sure the gospel link
isn't broken in your generation?

RAISING RELIABLE WITNESSES

As Samuel grew up, the LORD was with him, and everything Samuel said proved to be reliable.
1 SAMUEL 3:19 NLT

Samuel's mother, Hannah, was faithful to keep her promise to You, Lord, in delivering Samuel to the temple where he would serve You his entire life. And You were with Samuel, and everything Samuel said proved to be reliable.

Lord, I know that my family doesn't have to be in full-time Christian service for this to be true in our own lives. If we are as dedicated as Hannah in wanting our children to know You, then You will be with them, and everything they say will be reliable. Give me Hannah's faith and determination to do exactly that.

THINK ABOUT IT:

How can you set your children apart for the Lord right now so He can use them in special ways in the future? If He calls them into full-time Christian service, will you fully support that?

STAYING ON TRACK

And it came to pass, when Samuel was old,
that he made his sons judges over Israel.
Now the name of his firstborn was Joel; and
the name of his second, Abiah: they were
judges in Beersheba. And his sons walked
not in his ways, but turned aside after lucre,
and took bribes, and perverted judgment.
1 SAMUEL 8:1–3 KJV

Samuel started strong. He was raised in the faith, and he was in tune with You. And when he became old and unable to fulfill his office, he handed his duties off to his children; but the temptation of riches proved too much for them, and they succumbed to it. I never want to see this happen in my own family. May my children stand strong against worldly temptation as my wife and I release them. Keep the lessons we've taught them front and center in their minds.

THINK ABOUT IT:

No generation is temptation-proof, but what are you doing to set up your children to remain faithful?

DO NOT TURN AWAY

"Do not be afraid," Samuel [said to the people of Israel who had asked for a king and realized the error of their way]. "You have done all this evil; yet do not turn away from the Lord, but serve the Lord with all your heart. Do not turn away after useless idols. They can do you no good, nor can they rescue you, because they are useless."
1 Samuel 12:20–21

Lord, my children are going to make bad choices at some point in their lives. When they do, may they turn toward You, rather than away from You, to confess their sin and then serve You with all their heart. As humans, we tend to hide our sin and stay away from You for extended periods, but this is not what Samuel encourages in today's verses, and surely, it's not what You want.

THINK ABOUT IT:

After your children have made poor decisions, how quick are they to return to the Lord? How can you help them?

SOUL TIES

Now it came about when he had finished speaking to Saul, that the soul of Jonathan was knit to the soul of David, and Jonathan loved him as himself.
1 SAMUEL 18:1 NASB

David and Jonathan had a friendship for the ages—one that always put the other person's needs, wants, and interests first, at any cost. We all need such friendships. Jesus had Peter, James, and John, and a few others. I have two or three similar friends. Bring this type of friendship into my children's lives, and make them desirous of being this type of friend to others. For such friendships last a lifetime and will see them through many trials, even after my wife and I are in heaven.

THINK ABOUT IT:

How can you help your children choose good friendships? What sort of characteristics should they be looking for and exhibiting themselves?

GOD WON'T FORGET

*For God is not unjust. He will not forget
how hard you have worked for him and
how you have shown your love to him by
caring for other believers, as you still do.*
HEBREWS 6:10 NLT

Lord, one of the ways Your Word says that
we show our love for You is by our dedication
to Your body of believers here on earth. You
emphasize the importance of caring for other
Christians because You identify so closely with
Your Church. Give my children a deep love for
Your Church; I'm not talking about a building
or programs, but instead, about Your people.
May my children never know a time when they
aren't surrounded by many Christians who know
and love them and are willing to invest in them.

THINK ABOUT IT:

What are you doing to make sure your children
are surrounded by Christians who love them?

HIGHER REGARD FOR OTHERS

*Do nothing from selfishness or empty conceit,
but with humility of mind regard one another
as more important than yourselves; do
not merely look out for your own personal
interests, but also for the interests of others.*
PHILIPPIANS 2:3–4 NASB

Father, in America, we often talk about our rights as American citizens, but we aren't nearly as quick to talk about the rights of others, or to consider other people as more important than we are. But Your Word calls us to a higher standard—one of humility—that looks out for the interests of others, even above our own interests. Remind me of this again and again as I think about my own wants and rights. I want to model today's verses for my children so they can see it in action.

THINK ABOUT IT:

If someone asked your children whether you place a higher value on your rights and interests than those of others, how would they respond?

THE OVERCOMER

"These things I have spoken to you, that in Me you may have peace. In the world you will have tribulation; but be of good cheer, I have overcome the world."
JOHN 16:33 NKJV

As Jesus prepared His disciples for His death and their subsequent dispersion, He wanted them to understand that tribulation in this world is the norm but to be of good cheer because He overcame the world. His disciples encountered the possibility of torture and death for their faith, but it was possible for them to be of good cheer because they finally understood that this world wasn't their home. They were headed to heaven for all eternity, where they would praise Christ day and night. May I have such an attitude among my family when tribulation comes in my own life.

THINK ABOUT IT:

How closely tied to this world are you? Can you be of good cheer during the most trying of times because you know they are temporary?

THE SAME SPIRIT

*But if the Spirit of him that raised up Jesus
from the dead dwell in you, he that raised up
Christ from the dead shall also quicken your
mortal bodies by his Spirit that dwelleth in you.*
ROMANS 8:11 KJV

Father, while my physical body is under the sentence of death because of sin, I agree with what Matthew Henry says in his commentary about this verse: "Grace in the soul is its new nature; the life of the saint lies in the soul, while the life of the sinner goes no further than the body." That grace in my soul allows me to shun the cravings of my flesh. Lord, remind me of this every time I'm tempted to obey the flesh, so I can show my children how to live this Christian life.

THINK ABOUT IT:

What sins were you able to give up instantly after conversion? Which ones do you still struggle with? How can Romans 8:11 help with the latter?

THE HIDDEN WORD

*I have hidden your word in my heart
that I might not sin against you.*
PSALM 119:11

Father, the surest way for me to avoid sinning against You is to hide Your Word in my heart. I know that involves going deep into Your precepts and then memorizing them. The Word needs to be the continual subject of my thoughts—more than work, more than sports, more than my entertainment plans. In fact, I need to continually bring Your Word to bear in all of these areas.

Surround me with friends who love Your Word and who inspire me to stay in it; and may I do the same for them. Allow my children to "catch me" in the Word on a regular basis so they know how much I treasure it.

THINK ABOUT IT:

What is your natural first line of defense against sin? How close of a correlation do you see between your walk with the Lord and the amount of time you spend in His Word?

WALK WITH THE WISE

Walk with the wise and become wise,
for a companion of fools suffers harm.
PROVERBS 13:20

Father, I know I need to be around wise people, but often I feel intimidated because of my lack of knowledge. But I'm drawn to them anyway. The books they read and the programs they watch intrigue me. The discussions they have afterward draw me in even more. Grant me the humility to approach such people, for it's the only way I'll become wiser. And it's the only way I'll become a wise mentor myself.

I want to be the type of father whose children approach him even when they are adults because they see wisdom in him. So grow me, Lord. Point me to the right people.

THINK ABOUT IT:

Are you considered the wisest person among your group of friends? If so, consider adding a friend or two—people who are wiser who can challenge your thinking.

SHINE

*The light shines in the darkness, and the
darkness can never extinguish it.*
JOHN 1:5 NLT

Father, sometimes I'm given to despair as I look
at the events taking place around the world, in
my city, and even in my own family. The world
is such a dark place—full of unthinkable crimes.
But You didn't call me to solve every problem. You do call me to shine my light in the darkness. As I do, darkness can never extinguish it.

In a blackout, one lit candle illuminates an
entire living room with enough light for an entire
family to see one another. More lit candles means
even more light. May our family shine brightly in
the darkness, Lord, so that the world can see You.

THINK ABOUT IT:

Are you given to despair over current events
in the world or in your family? How can today's
verse change your perspective?

GOD PLEASERS

For am I now seeking the favor of men, or of
God? Or am I striving to please men?
If I were still trying to please men,
I would not be a bond-servant of Christ.
GALATIANS 1:10 NASB

Just as the apostle Paul fought for the purity of
the gospel in Galatia as the church there began
to abandon it in favor of traditions, I too want to
maintain its purity in my family. May we never bow
to the whims of culture or even to the traditions
of men in the Church. By striving to always please
You rather than man, we may step on some toes.
I only ask that You give us a spirit of humility as
we do so. For to become people pleasers would
mean we were not bond servants of Christ. May
that never be the case.

THINK ABOUT IT:

Do you feel pressure from your church body
to conform to traditions that detract from the
gospel? How willing are you to hold the line?

HEEDING CORRECTION

Whoever heeds life-giving correction will be at home among the wise. Those who disregard discipline despise themselves, but the one who heeds correction gains understanding.
PROVERBS 15:31–32

The notion of being corrected often makes my skin crawl, Lord. It's embarrassing and humiliating but so necessary for my sanctification. The writer of today's verses refers to "life-giving correction," which seems to mean this correction leads to spiritual life, in that, as I walk in the truth, I'm infused with power from on high. How could I ever resist such a thing?

Disregarding discipline is foolish on my part. Not only is it harmful in the here and now, but doing so also damages my soul.

Make me open to life-giving correction, Lord, that I may walk closer with You.

THINK ABOUT IT:

What's your first reaction when a wise person corrects you? Is it a godly, life-giving reaction? Or are you defensive?

JOYFUL WORSHIP

*Come, let us sing to the Lord! Let us shout
joyfully to the Rock of our salvation.
Let us come to him with thanksgiving.
Let us sing psalms of praise to him.*
PSALM 95:1–2 NLT

Lord, I want to teach my children to praise You with a joyful noise—even if I'm uncomfortable doing so. I've seen several reports in recent years about men not being active participants in worship, and I think about the effect that will have on my children if I am one of them. I'm willing to raise my hands in victory at a football or baseball game, so how much more willing ought I to be in showing such exuberance when worshipping You, the one true God?

THINK ABOUT IT:

Were you raised in a church environment that frowned on shouting joyfully to the Rock of your salvation? Are you willing to obey today's verses rather than your tradition?

OPPORTUNITY FOR SERVICE

Therefore, as we have opportunity,
let us do good to all, especially to those
who are of the household of faith.
GALATIANS 6:10 NKJV

Father, You identify so closely with Your Church that You tell us to pay special attention to those who are in the household of faith. As I go about my day, remind me of ways I can do just that—whether it's a text to let someone know I'm praying about his situation, or taking people out for coffee to learn more about them or how I can serve them. I know that I let too many such opportunities slip by without following through, but I don't want to do that anymore.

Also, make my children sensitive to the needs of other Christians. May they look for ways to reach out.

THINK ABOUT IT:

How can you better serve the Church (not necessarily within the four walls) on a regular basis?

REAL FRIENDS

There are "friends" who destroy each other,
but a real friend sticks closer than a brother.
PROVERBS 18:24 NLT

Father, we often say that blood is thicker than water, but in today's verse, Your Word says a real friend sticks closer than a brother. I need that type of friend in my life so I can be the husband and father You call me to be.

And please bring real friends into the lives of my children—friends who are willing to encourage them in their faith, pick them up when they are down, and challenge them when they are wrong. They need friends who will never walk away from them or take advantage of them. I pray for lifers, Father—friends who will be with them until death parts them.

THINK ABOUT IT:

Can you name one or two friends who feel closer than a brother to you? How about your children? Are they developing friendships like that?

SPEAK UP

*With my mouth will I make known Your
faithfulness to all generations.*
PSALM 89:1 NKJV

While the men of my generation are more open
than previous generations to talk about what we
think and believe, I still don't find it to be easy,
Lord. But the generations in my family need to
know about Your faithfulness, and I want them to
hear it from me. So, with my mouth, I will make
it known. Now I ask for ample opportunities.

May I speak about Your faithfulness at the
dinner table, at cheerleading or soccer practice,
on vacation—anywhere that allows for natural
conversation. Provide teachable moments in
our lives and make me fully aware of them, Lord,
so I can take full advantage. And as my children
mature and eventually marry, may I be just as
diligent to speak about You to their children.

THINK ABOUT IT:

When was the last time you spoke about God's
faithfulness to the generations in your family?
How can you improve?

REMEMBER HIS PRECEPTS

But the lovingkindness of the Lord is from everlasting to everlasting on those who fear Him, and His righteousness to children's children, to those who keep His covenant and remember His precepts to do them.
PSALM 103:17–18 NASB

In the West, we tend to think individualistically, Lord. We don't always think about Your covenant and the blessing it brings as we raise our children in the faith. But Your loving-kindness is from everlasting to everlasting—from one generation to the next. That's the way the faith has always been passed on.

Thank You for Your faithfulness when we are unfaithful. Thank You for loving us when we are so unlovable. Remind us of Your precepts every day so that we may continue to keep Your covenant from one generation to the next.

THINK ABOUT IT:

What are you doing to teach your children and your children's children the precepts of God? What does it look like, practically speaking?

YOUR FAITH HERITAGE

I am writing to you, fathers, because you know Him who has been from the beginning. I am writing to you, young men, because you have overcome the evil one. I have written to you, children, because you know the Father.
1 JOHN 2:13 NASB

Lord, I want this to be the legacy of my family—even if my own father didn't know You from the beginning. My generation can become the hinge generation—the one where everything changes. But even if my father knew You, we want to go deeper with each generation. May there come a time in my bloodline in which a generation can say it never knew a time when our family wasn't faithful to You. They can forget me, Father, but may they never forget You.

THINK ABOUT IT:

How far back can you trace your faith heritage? If you can go back several generations, do your children know the stories of how those generations came to saving faith?

PRAISE HIM NOW

For the grave cannot praise you, death cannot sing your praise; those who go down to the pit cannot hope for your faithfulness. The living, the living—they praise you, as I am doing today; parents tell their children about your faithfulness.
ISAIAH 38:18–19

Father, Your Word tells us we "are destined to die once, and after that to face judgment" (Hebrews 9:27). It also says, "Our days may come to seventy years, or eighty, if our strength endures; yet the best of them are but trouble and sorrow, for they quickly pass, and we fly away" (Psalm 90:10).

We have such limited time to praise You and to tell our children about You. We cannot do so from the grave, so give me the focus and opportunities to do it now.

THINK ABOUT IT:

Do your children know the ways God has been faithful to you and your wife through the years? If not, praise Him now while you still have breath.

HEAVENLY MINDED

*Join together in following my example,
brothers and sisters, and just as you have
us as a model, keep your eyes on those who
live as we do. For, as I have often told you
before and now tell you again even with tears,
many live as enemies of the cross of Christ.*
PHILIPPIANS 3:17–18

Father, the apostle Paul wanted the Philippian church to model itself after its mature members (v. 15) so they could avoid following their natural appetites. Instead, they set their minds on earthly things (v. 19). I know my children will make poor decisions sometimes and ultimately sin, much like I have, but may those instances be brief. Help us to put our old self to death so we can no longer hear its destructive voice.

THINK ABOUT IT:

If your children were to mimic your current lifestyle, would they be following their natural appetites, or would they be focused on things above?

A PRUDENT SPOUSE

Houses and wealth are inherited from parents,
but a prudent wife is from the LORD.
PROVERBS 19:14

Leaving an inheritance for my children is a good thing—a biblical thing—but there is something that is more important: finding a prudent spouse. I know that my children's spouses will come directly from You. May it be so, Father. May my children consider candidates for marriage based on Christian character—people who are marked by prudence, who are careful and sensible and have sound judgment in the faith. Looks will fade, but prudence will remain constant.

Make these candidates clear for my children. I don't want them to fret about who they will marry or when they will marry. Help them to convey a total trust in You and Your providence. It will happen at the right time and the right place as they trust in You.

THINK ABOUT IT:

What is your typical advice for your children when it comes to marriage? What characteristics do you tell them to watch for?

EXHIBIT PATIENCE

*And, ye fathers, provoke not your children
to wrath: but bring them up in the
nurture and admonition of the Lord.*
EPHESIANS 6:4 KJV

Lord, You have entrusted me with authority over my children. May I always remember that. You didn't give them to me to serve me. Instead, You gave them to me to raise them in the faith and then release them into the world to do what You've called them to do. As I'm patient and nurturing with them, they get a small glimpse of You.

Sometimes I'll need to reprove them, but I always want to do so in a loving manner so I don't provoke them to wrath. Give me the words and the approach I need to keep them on the right track without crushing their spirits.

THINK ABOUT IT:

Are you willing to ask your wife if you've ever provoked your children to wrath? If you have, are you willing to ask them for forgiveness and a fresh start?

IMITATE GOD

*Imitate God, therefore, in everything you do,
because you are his dear children. Live a life
filled with love, following the example of Christ.
He loved us and offered himself as a sacrifice
for us, a pleasing aroma to God. Let there be no
sexual immorality, impurity, or greed among you.
Such sins have no place among God's people.*
EPHESIANS 5:1–3 NLT

Father, I know that children imitate their parents,
for better or worse. May I imitate You daily so my
children will imitate You. And when I fall short,
may I be quick to repent. I want my children to
see the reality of my faith. I want them to see
how You prompt me to love others, even difficult
people. And I want them to see me guarding my
heart and eyes from sexual immorality, impurity,
and greed. This is pleasing to You, and it is also
the example my children deserve.

THINK ABOUT IT:

When was the last time your children saw or
heard you repent?

BEFORE GOD'S FACE

In the early morning, while it was still dark,
Jesus got up, left the house, and went away
to a secluded place, and was praying there.
MARK 1:35 NASB

The day after Jesus healed and taught many, He rose early to find a place to pray. His soul earnestly desired connection with You, Father, and that drove Him out of bed while it was still dark and quiet. That's what I want our relationship to look like. That's why I'm here with You this morning. Quiet my soul, and turn it toward heaven. Help me block out any distractions going on around me so I can hear from You. The concerns of the day will be upon me soon enough, but not before I've spent time before Your face.

THINK ABOUT IT:

Are you driven out of bed each morning with a compulsion to seek the Lord?

STORE DURING THE SUMMER

There are four things on earth that are small but unusually wise: Ants—they aren't strong, but they store up food all summer.
Proverbs 30:24–25 NLT

In a culture in which entitlement and instant gratification are the norm, I want my children to know and understand the wisdom of the ants, Lord. They aren't the strongest insect, but they have a strong work ethic. They store up food all summer, knowing that winter is coming. May my children have a similarly strong work ethic, knowing they have a limited amount of time to store resources for their latter years. They don't have to necessarily be strong or prestigious to do so. Help me to convey this truth to them.

THINK ABOUT IT:

If your children were to describe your work ethic, what would they say? Do you complain about going to work each day, or do you convey a spirit of thankfulness for the work?

DWELLING IN SAFETY

There are four things on earth that are small but unusually wise. . . . Hyraxes [a small furry animal that is also referred to as a rock rabbit, rock badger, or field mouse]—they aren't powerful, but they make their homes among the rocks.
PROVERBS 30:24, 26 NLT

Father, just as hyraxes, which aren't powerful animals, build their houses in rocks where they can be protected from the elements and predators, may my children learn to burrow into You for protection. First Peter 5:8 (NLT) says, "Stay alert! Watch out for your great enemy, the devil. He prowls around like a roaring lion, looking for someone to devour." While I know it isn't possible for them to always avoid Satan and his ploys, I also know that the closer they are to You, the less likely they are to fall prey to him.

THINK ABOUT IT:

When you face difficult circumstances, how quick are you to run to God rather than trying to change your circumstances?

STAYING IN LINE

There are four things on earth that are small but unusually wise. . . . Locusts—they have no king, but they march in formation.
PROVERBS 30:24, 27 NLT

In Matthew Henry's commentary, he says locusts go forth "like an army in battle-array; and, observing such good order among themselves, it is not any inconvenience to them that they have no king." Such behavior is their natural instinct. The scriptures call this behavior wise.

Father, we know that the Christian shouldn't need a king or a boss or an overseer to stay in line in service to You, but yet we often stray out of line. May my children see a willingness in me to honor You in all that I do, regardless of whether anybody else is watching or not.

THINK ABOUT IT:

In what ways do you resemble the actions of a locust, as described in today's verse? Why do you think the scripture calls this action wise?

PERSIST DURING ADVERSITY

There are four things on earth that are small but unusually wise. . . . Lizards [some translations say "spiders"]—they are easy to catch, but they are found even in kings' palaces.
PROVERBS 30:24, 28 NLT

Father, as much as humans try to exterminate spiders, they can be found everywhere—in the homes of the poor and the rich. It's a lesson in persistence. Those who are willing to do what You put in front of them will eventually find success—not in the worldly sense, but in the spiritual sense. Just as a spider uncomplainingly rebuilds its web when the rain wipes it away, so should be our attitude about ministry, no matter the challenges we face.

THINK ABOUT IT:

When you hit a spiritual roadblock, are you quick to complain or quit? How can you be more like the spider that accepts rebuilding without complaint?

DELIGHTING IN GOD'S LAW

*Blessed is the one who does not walk in step
with the wicked or stand in the way that sinners
take or sit in the company of mockers, but
whose delight is in the law of the LORD, and
who meditates on his law day and night.*
PSALM 1:1–2

Today's verses describe the heart of a godly person. Such a person finds fulfillment in delighting in Your law—by meditating on it day and night. This is a far cry, Father, from simply snacking on the Word in the morning or evening but then going about my life without giving it a further thought. Permeate my mind with Your Word. Give me an insatiable hunger for it. And may my family see that and follow suit so they can avoid walking with the wicked.

THINK ABOUT IT:

What does your daily Bible reading look like? Is it devotional in nature? Do you also study the Bible or memorize it?

WHAT IS MANKIND?

When I consider your heavens, the work of your fingers, the moon and the stars, which you have set in place, what is mankind that you are mindful of them, human beings that you care for them?
PSALM 8:3–4

Father, one of the best ways I know to marvel over Your power and majesty is to be mindful of my surroundings—especially in nature. My naked eye can only see a limited number of stars, but Your hand hung them all. As I contemplate the size of the universe and the way it runs, in spite of the fall, I can't help but ask the same question David asked in today's verses: What is mankind that You are mindful of us? But yet, You love us. Help me pass on this big-picture perspective to my children.

THINK ABOUT IT:

Estimates vary, but there are between 100–400 million stars just in our galaxy. How many can you see? How does this bring perspective for today's verses?

THE LORD REIGNS

The LORD reigns forever; he has established his throne for judgment. He rules the world in righteousness and judges the peoples with equity.
PSALM 9:7–8

Lord, I want my children to grow up with a passion for justice, but I want it to be rooted in Your Word. When we consider the injustices we see in this world, it's easy to fall into the trap of believing that everything is random and that You are not in control, but Your Word says something much different. You reign forever and have established Your throne. You rule the world in righteousness and judge with equity. Even when our family doesn't see evidence of this, may we always be mindful of it—speaking it to one another as a reminder.

THINK ABOUT IT:

What do you tell your children when they ask you about the injustices they see on television or in school? How does your answer compare with today's verses?

BEAUTY IS FLEETING

Charm is deceptive, and beauty is fleeting; but
*a woman who fears the L*ORD *is to be praised.*
PROVERBS 31:30

Lord, I want my children to have the right priorities. I want them to focus much more on building their character and seeking out people of high character than on allowing themselves to be deceived by beauty. This applies to both friendships and seeking a spouse. A woman who fears You is to be praised. The same can be said of a man. Physical beauty is fleeting, but inner beauty lasts a lifetime. But this is difficult for all of us to embrace, Father, for we are sinful. That's all the more reason why I need to persevere in teaching my children biblical principles for all of life.

THINK ABOUT IT:

Do your children hear you comment about the physical beauty of people more than they hear you speaking about a person's fear of the Lord?

FINISHING WELL

*"But I do not consider my life of any account
as dear to myself, so that I may finish my
course and the ministry which I received
from the Lord Jesus, to testify solemnly
of the gospel of the grace of God."*
ACTS 20:24 NASB

I don't want to be the kind of father who considers his life, his hobbies, and his desires to be so dear that I fail to finish the ministry You've given me. Fatherhood is my highest earthly priority. You've entrusted my children to my care for a brief period of time with the instruction that I'm to train them in Your ways as I testify solemnly of the gospel of the grace of God. May I be ever diligent in doing so.

THINK ABOUT IT:

How are your children doing spiritually? How can you guide them in grace to an even deeper walk with the Lord?

BE STRONG AND COURAGEOUS

"Have I not commanded you? Be strong and courageous! Do not tremble or be dismayed, for the LORD your God is with you wherever you go."
JOSHUA 1:9 NASB

After the death of Moses, You commissioned Joshua to lead Israel across the Jordan and into the Promised Land. You told him to "be strong and courageous, for you shall give this people possession of the land which I swore to their fathers to give them" (v. 6 NASB). The Israelites weren't to tremble or be dismayed in the face of the unknown.

Our own country is becoming a foreign land to us, Father, in the sense that our culture is embracing debauchery. As we cross the Jordan, may we, as a family, be strong and courageous as we seek to live counterculturally to maintain our saltiness.

THINK ABOUT IT:

Are you strong and courageous in your approach to engaging the culture? Would your wife and children agree with your self-assessment?

WALKING BLAMELESSLY

LORD, who may dwell in your sacred tent? Who may live on your holy mountain? The one whose walk is blameless, who does what is righteous, who speaks the truth from their heart.
PSALM 15:1–2

In this psalm, David openly wonders about the type of person who will be allowed into heaven. Lord, I know that salvation is by grace alone and that a laundry list of godly characteristics cannot save me, but I should also see evidence of such characteristics in my life and in my family.

John Wesley said that those whose walk is blameless love and serve God, as well as their neighbor, not only in word but also in truth, on a continual basis. And "his words and professions to God and men, agree with the thoughts and purposes of his heart."

THINK ABOUT IT:

Today's verses talk about a consistent walk with Christ. How consistent is your walk with Him?

TAMING THE TONGUE

Lord, who may dwell in your sacred tent? Who may live on your holy mountain? . . . [The one] whose tongue utters no slander, who does no wrong to a neighbor, and casts no slur on others.
Psalm 15:1, 3

As David continues to investigate the character of the godly person who is heaven-bound, he mentions the proper treatment of others. Taming our tongue is difficult but necessary to keep from slandering someone's character. Help me to tame my tongue, Father. Treating my neighbors well is something I struggle with when they aren't mindful of others, but give me the grace to do so anyway. Slurs on others easily roll off my tongue sometimes—usually to make myself feel better. Kill my urge to do so, Father. May I hold no animosity toward others in light of my own sin.

THINK ABOUT IT:

What is your first reaction when someone wrongs you or says something bad about you? Rather than striking back, how might you better defuse the situation?

HANDLING A VILE PERSON

Lord, who may dwell in your sacred tent? Who may live on your holy mountain? . . . [The one] who despises a vile person but honors those who fear the Lord; who keeps an oath even when it hurts, and does not change their mind.
PSALM 15:1, 4

Lord, sometimes I struggle to understand Your Word, and today's verses provide one such instance. A godly person is called to despise a vile person. At the same time, I know I am to love my enemies, who are often vile people. Bible commentator Adam Clarke offers this insight: "This man judges of others by their conduct; he tries no man's heart." In that sense I understand, for I too fall short.

David also speaks of a godly person keeping his oath and not being prone to changing his mind.

May I be all of these things, Lord.

THINK ABOUT IT:

Are you able to judge others by their conduct while leaving their heart to God?

HELPING THE POOR

LORD, who may dwell in your sacred tent?
Who may live on your holy mountain? . . .
[The one] who lends money to the poor
without interest; who does not accept
a bribe against the innocent.
PSALM 15:1, 5

Lord, You tell us many times in the scriptures to be sensitive to the needs of the poor. Here in today's verses, You tell us to lend money to the poor without interest, for the poor have a difficult enough lot without having to pay interest. Whenever I have an opportunity to make such a loan, give me the heart to do so—one that wants to help without seeing any personal benefit.

Today's verses also say to not accept a bribe against the innocent. This may apply to situations when we would defend a wealthier person simply because we have more to gain financially. May that never be the case with my family, Lord.

THINK ABOUT IT:

Have your children seen you help the poor without any expectation of personal gain?

A SECURED LOT

LORD, you alone are my portion and my cup; you make my lot secure. The boundary lines have fallen for me in pleasant places; surely I have a delightful inheritance.
PSALM 16:5–6

Just as the Levitical priests had no inheritance in the Promised Land and were told that God was their portion, so it is with Christians. God calls us to be satisfied and delighted with the portion that He provides—no matter how big or small that may be. Examine my heart, oh Lord, and see if You find any dissatisfaction in me regarding my portion. If so, root it out so I can be a model for my children.

THINK ABOUT IT:

Have you and your wife been caught up in the upsizing game in search of satisfaction and security? If so, what message might that be sending to your kids? How do these verses challenge you to live differently?

THE COMPASSIONATE FATHER

*As a father has compassion on his children,
so the LORD has compassion on those
who fear him; for he knows how we are
formed, he remembers that we are dust.*
PSALM 103:13–14

Father, You paint a perfect picture of parenthood in today's verses. We know that You love us, Your children, and that no matter how far we sometimes stray from You, You don't love us any less. You know our weaknesses because You Yourself formed us. May I always remember this example as I deal with my own children, who sometimes stray and disappoint me. I want them to remember me as a man of compassion—one who understands weakness because I myself am weak.

THINK ABOUT IT:

If your children were asked to describe you in one word, with nobody else around, what would each of them say? How might their hypothetical answers drive you to change?

SINGLED OUT

"I have singled him [Abraham] out so that he will direct his sons and their families to keep the way of the LORD by doing what is right and just. Then I will do for Abraham all that I have promised."
GENESIS 18:19 NLT

With the judgment of Sodom and Gomorrah at hand for their flagrant sin (v. 20), You, Lord, singled out Abraham to direct his family in keeping Your way, promising to make his descendants more bountiful than the stars.

Father, in a similar manner, You choose fathers in the new covenant to direct their families to keep Your way rather than bending to the whims of culture. I want to allow my children to ask the hard questions, while always steering them back to You and Your Word.

THINK ABOUT IT:

Who is the spiritual leader of your home? If it isn't you, is it because you have been negligent? Are you willing to express a desire to take back the reins in a loving manner?

MAKING GOD KNOWN

For He established a testimony in Jacob, and appointed a law in Israel, which He commanded our fathers, that they should make them known to their children; that the generation to come might know them, the children who would be born, that they may arise and declare them to their children.

PSALM 78:5–6 NKJV

Father, making Your commands known to my children so that the generation to come might know them is the passion of my heart. I confess that it hasn't always been the case. But I want my children's children to know You. And I know that only happens if I'm diligent in introducing You to my own children. We quickly forget the names and faces of generations past, but a legacy of faith in Christ endures, regardless.

THINK ABOUT IT:

Can you name your great-grandfather or great-grandmother? Do you know what they believed? Or didn't believe?

FULL OF DAYS

After this Job lived one hundred and forty years, and saw his children and grandchildren for four generations. So Job died, old and full of days.
JOB 42:16–17 NKJV

After Job experienced great loss and was dressed down by the Lord for asking rather presumptuous questions, he repented. And Lord, You restored him, allowing him to see his children and grandchildren for four generations.

Oh, how I wish to see the generations to follow. I confess to committing many great sins, but I learned from Job. I never want to ask presumptuous questions of You. I simply want to die old and full of days, satisfied in knowing my family is full of Christ followers. And before I do, may they come to me for encouragement in the faith. Then I'll be ready to enter my rest.

THINK ABOUT IT:

When you consider your latter days, what do you think about? Have you ever considered asking God to allow you to see multiple generations in your family?

THE GREATEST JOY

*I have no greater joy than to hear
that my children walk in truth.*
3 JOHN 1:4 NKJV

Just as John wrote to Gaius—who was probably a convert under John's teaching—and expressed his great joy over hearing that his spiritual children were walking in truth, I too find no greater joy in this life, Father.

Thank You for giving me such glimpses into the spiritual lives of my children and those who have come to the faith under my teaching. For a steadfast walk with You is good evidence of Your Spirit at work inside them. Give me more such glimpses, Lord, because they testify of Your love and faithfulness. And spur me on to continue the ministry You've given me in their lives.

THINK ABOUT IT:

What is your greatest joy in life? Does it have anything to do with seeing God's Spirit at work in someone you've ministered to in some fashion?

CRYING OUT TO GOD

*In my distress I called to the L*ORD*; I cried to my God for help. From his temple he heard my voice; my cry came before him, into his ears.*
PSALM 18:6

When David was surrounded by his enemies, he called to You, oh Lord. He didn't turn to the hundreds of men he had with him to rescue him. He didn't depend on his own strength or wisdom. And when he called on You, You heard him.

That's the kind of faith I want to exhibit to my family. May I not turn to friends or my own wisdom first when I'm in crisis, but instead may I call on You. In reality, who else could I turn to? You are omnipresent, omnipotent, and ever loving—the all-perfect God who loves me.

THINK ABOUT IT:

What is your first instinct when you are in crisis? Do you reach out to friends? Do you pull away from everybody? Or do you call on God?

HOW MUCH MORE?

"Or what man is there among you who, when his son asks for a loaf, will give him a stone? Or if he asks for a fish, he will not give him a snake, will he? If you then, being evil, know how to give good gifts to your children, how much more will your Father who is in heaven give what is good to those who ask Him!"

MATTHEW 7:9–11 NASB

Father, just like Jesus said in today's verses, I do everything I can to meet the needs and even desires of my children because I love them. But the bigger lesson here is that You go above and beyond for Your children, incomparable to anything I could ever do in my sinful state. Remembering this should stop me from ever questioning Your love for me when I ask You for something. You are perfect. You are holy. And You know exactly what I need. Thank You, Lord.

THINK ABOUT IT:

Do today's verses increase your faith in God?

SPIRITUAL GROUNDWORK

When the days of feasting had completed their cycle, Job would send and consecrate them [Job's children], rising up early in the morning and offering burnt offerings according to the number of them all; for Job said, "Perhaps my sons have sinned and cursed God in their hearts." Thus Job did continually.

JOB 1:5 NASB

Job's spiritual concern for his children ran so deep that he rose early in the morning to pray for them. "Not that he did or could make them holy, by imparting grace, or infusing holiness into them; at most he could only pray for their sanctification, and give them rules, precepts, and instructions about holiness, and exhortations to it," says John Gill in his commentary.

This is the type of father I want to be—one who lays the spiritual groundwork for his children.

THINK ABOUT IT:

Do you make it a habit of rising early to pray for your children by name, and maybe even by sin?

EXAMINE MY HEART, LORD

But who can discern their own errors? Forgive my hidden faults. Keep your servant also from willful sins; may they not rule over me. Then I will be blameless, innocent of great transgression.
PSALM 19:12–13

Father, as I consider my known sins, they grieve me. But what man can know his hidden faults—the ones buried deep inside that lead him astray? I pray with David this morning, asking You to keep me from willful sins so they don't rule over me. And root out my hidden sins too, Lord. I know I'll never achieve perfection, but my earnest desire is to walk with You, innocent of great transgression.

THINK ABOUT IT:

When your children are grown and on their own, will they remember you as a father who was willing to examine his own heart and then was quick to repent?

LEAVING AN INHERITANCE

A good man leaves an inheritance to his children's children, but the wealth of the sinner is stored up for the righteous.
PROVERBS 13:22 NKJV

As much as we are called not to love money, You do call me to provide for my family and also to build enough of a nest egg to provide for my children's children. When I reflect on that, it means I not only need to work hard, but I also need to be frugal in storing money for the extended future. And I need to teach my children those same principles if their children are to see any benefit. May I honor You with every dollar I make and save, knowing You will use it long after You've called me home.

THINK ABOUT IT:

Are you living in such a fashion as to be obedient to today's verse? What changes can you make, starting today?

CHASTENING IN LOVE

If you endure chastening, God deals with you as with sons; for what son is there whom a father does not chasten? But if you are without chastening, of which all have become partakers, then you are illegitimate and not sons.
HEBREWS 12:7–8 NKJV

Father, Your Word says chastening is to be expected as a child of God. In fact, those who aren't chastened are illegitimate and do not belong to You. Likewise, I chasten my own children because I love them, even though they don't always see it that way. Give me the wisdom to know when to step in and when to back off. And when the situation calls for chastening, may I do so swiftly but also in love.

THINK ABOUT IT:

Do you discipline out of anger or maybe because your children don't live up to your expectations? Or do you discipline in love in an attempt to keep your children focused on the narrow road?

SHARP ARROWS

Children are a gift from the L<small>ORD</small>; they are a reward from him. Children born to a young man are like arrows in a warrior's hands. How joyful is the man whose quiver is full of them!
P<small>SALM</small> 127:3–5 <small>NLT</small>

Lord, I do indeed consider my children a gift from above. And I want to train them to be like arrows in a warrior's hands. That means they need to be sharp spiritually, able to pierce the darkness with truth. And they need to be sturdy, able to endure a turbulent flight path. May our home be a training ground for such arrows—a place of safety where they can ask the tough questions so they are fully prepared for battle. I can think of nothing better than opening my door and sending such arrows out into the world.

THINK ABOUT IT:

What does your training ground look like? What are you doing to prepare your children spiritually for the darkness they will face once they step out on their own?

REDEEM THE TIME

Make the most of every opportunity in these evil days. Don't act thoughtlessly, but understand what the Lord wants you to do.
EPHESIANS 5:16–17 NLT

Lord, as my children grow into young adults, they will be faced with so many allurements in this day and age—from consumerism, to drugs and alcohol, to fornication. May they make the most of every opportunity that they have to redeem the time.

In verses 18–19 (NLT), Paul explains what this ought to look like: "Don't be drunk with wine, because that will ruin your life. Instead, be filled with the Holy Spirit, singing psalms and hymns and spiritual songs among yourselves, and making music to the Lord in your hearts."

May my children stay engaged in Christian community, and may that community build one another up in the faith.

THINK ABOUT IT:

How much emphasis do you place on helping your children find and stay in Christian community?

THE PATH OF LIFE

You make known to me the path of life; you will fill me with joy in your presence, with eternal pleasures at your right hand.
PSALM 16:11

Father, I trust You with my family's future. Sometimes I struggle to know which path to take. Knowing which job to take, which house to buy, which city to live in, and which church to attend can feel overwhelming, but You are always in control, leading and guiding us. And as we depend on You, You fill us with joy in Your presence. Even when I don't have any sense of direction, give me a sense of peace and humble reliance on You as I wait for You to speak.

THINK ABOUT IT:

What does your major decision-making process look like? Do you weigh the pros and cons first? Or hold a family meeting? Or are you wholly dependent on God's leading?

PROVIDING FOR YOUR OWN

But if anyone does not provide for his own, and especially for those of his household, he has denied the faith and is worse than an unbeliever.
1 Timothy 5:8 NASB

The message of today's verse is a serious one—one that I personally take to heart, Father. I know that You call me to provide for my family by anticipating their needs and then working to meet them. So, according to my ability, I gladly accept my calling to do so, all the while being totally dependent on You to work out the details.

Providing for one's family is so serious that to do otherwise is a denial of the faith. For how can someone call himself a follower of Christ but then fail to care for his own?

THINK ABOUT IT:

Do you view work—any work—as godly and from the Lord as a way to provide for your family? If not, how might doing so change your attitude about it?

SUBDUING THE EARTH

God created man in His own image, in the image of God He created him; male and female He created them. God blessed them; and God said to them, "Be fruitful and multiply, and fill the earth, and subdue it; and rule over the fish of the sea and over the birds of the sky and over every living thing that moves on the earth."
GENESIS 1:27–28 NASB

Lord, I marvel over the fact that You made my family in Your image and that You gave us rule over fish, birds, cattle, and every creeping thing. Not every couple can have children, but in Your providence, You've told those who can to be fruitful and multiply to subdue the earth. Children are a gift from You (Psalm 127:3), and as we raise them in the fear and admonition of You, the gospel advances from one generation to the next.

THINK ABOUT IT:

How, specifically, is your family subduing the earth? Consider asking this question at dinner tonight.

THIRSTY LAND

"For I will pour water on the thirsty land, and streams on the dry ground; I will pour out my Spirit on your offspring, and my blessing on your descendants. They will spring up like grass in a meadow, like poplar trees by flowing streams."
ISAIAH 44:3–4

After God's people committed great sin (Isaiah 43), He wanted them to know His mercy would prevail in the midst of their thirsty land. He promised to pour out His Spirit on Israel's offspring and they would spring up like grass in a meadow.

Father, You are a covenant-keeping God—one who is faithful, even though we, Your people, are often not. Thank You for pouring out Your Spirit on my offspring and for planting them in this world for Your glory. This brings such joy to my heart.

THINK ABOUT IT:

Consider your most grievous sin. Now reread today's verses, understanding they were spoken to people in such a circumstance. How does this promise reassure your soul?

PURSUE RIGHTEOUS LIVING

Run from anything that stimulates youthful lusts.
Instead, pursue righteous living, faithfulness,
love, and peace. Enjoy the companionship of
those who call on the Lord with pure hearts.
2 TIMOTHY 2:22 NLT

Father, give me the strength to obey today's verse. I know it's not a onetime event but a daily decision. I need to surround myself with the companionship of those who call on You with pure hearts, for I cannot expect purity among those who aren't seeking it or, worse, mock it.

Second Timothy 2:21 says that if I keep myself pure, I will be a special utensil for honorable use, ready for You to use for every good work. I'm a willing subject, Father. And I want to model such a life for my family. So, I'm ready to obey this teaching.

THINK ABOUT IT:

If you are struggling during a season of sin, do you see a correlation between the amount of time you spend around God's people versus the time you spend alone?

HE SEES MY WAYS

"I made a covenant with my eyes not to look lustfully at a young woman. . . . Does he not see my ways and count my every step?"
JOB 31:1, 4

Father, I'm inspired by Job's words in today's verses. He knew the seriousness of straying eyes. Rather than trying to resist temptation, he made a promise to himself to not even look lustfully at a young woman because he knew You saw everything he did.

Lord, I make a similar covenant with my own eyes this morning not to look lustfully at women at work, at church, or anywhere else. Grant me the power to turn away the second my sinful heart starts to show an interest. I know I'll have to give an account for my actions someday, so empower me to triumph over my flesh.

THINK ABOUT IT:

Have you ever considered making such a covenant with your eyes until today? How might you hold yourself to it?

THE LORD'S ANOINTED

*Then Abishai said to David, "God has delivered
your enemy [Saul] into your hand this day. . . ."
But David said to Abishai, "Do not destroy
him; for who can stretch out his hand against
the LORD's anointed, and be guiltless?"*
1 SAMUEL 26:8–9 NKJV

Lord, Abishai misread the situation, believing
God had delivered Saul into David's hands when
David and his men approached Saul, who was
sleeping, after spying out the land. David rightly
acknowledged that Saul was God's anointed, so
he couldn't destroy him.

Romans 13 tells us to be subject to the gov-
erning authorities. They are Your anointed, Lord.
As a Christian, I may disagree with the policies
of our leaders, but I have to be careful about the
words I use when I disagree. I shall not assassinate
a leader's character and be held guiltless.

THINK ABOUT IT:

What sort of things do your children hear you
say about the president? Your senators? Your
mayor? Other leaders?

REMEMBERING THE LORD

*So it was, as soon as Gideon was dead, that
the children of Israel again played the harlot
with the Baals, and made Baal-Berith their god.
Thus the children of Israel did not remember the
LORD their God, who had delivered them from
the hands of all their enemies on every side.*
JUDGES 8:33–34 NKJV

Father, I'm quick to forget You when You deliver
me or my family from an illness, a dangerous
situation, or sin. As soon as You have done so,
we return to our normal routines, hardly giving
You a second thought. Forgive us, Father. May I
be the type of dad who has a long memory of Your
faithfulness—one who reminds his family again
and again how You've delivered us.

THINK ABOUT IT:

Have you ever considered keeping a journal to
record God-moments in your family's history?

READ EVERY WORD

There was not a word of all that Moses had commanded which Joshua did not read before all the assembly of Israel, with the women, the little ones, and the strangers who were living among them.

JOSHUA 8:35 NKJV

Father, as Joshua was renewing the covenant, he gathered everyone in Israel—the men, women, children, and foreigners—and read every word from the book of the law, a practice that was to occur every seven years (Deuteronomy 31:10–11). He didn't skip over even the minutest detail, knowing it was all relevant.

I want to be a Joshua to my family—one who reads the Word to them continually so they don't forget what it says. And I want to do it for myself as well, because I'm just as prone to wander. May we cover every portion of the scriptures at some point.

THINK ABOUT IT:

How much of your family devotion time is spent on simply reading the Word out loud?

ENTERING THE ARK

*Then the LORD said to Noah, "Come into
the ark, you and all your household,
because I have seen that you are righteous
before Me in this generation."*
GENESIS 7:1 NKJV

Even when the entire world has turned against
You, Lord, it is possible to stand for You. Make
me like Noah—a man who was willing to obey
Your voice when everyone around him must have
thought he was crazy. And when I fail You, may
I be quick to repent and turn back toward You.
Usher my household into the ark of heaven, Lord,
at Your appointed time. Not because we are
righteous in and of ourselves, but because You
are our righteousness and apart from You we
would be wholly undeserving.

THINK ABOUT IT:

How has the Lord asked your family to stand
out from your neighbors? How willing have you
been to obey?

HINDERED PRAYERS

*Husbands, in the same way be considerate
as you live with your wives, and treat them
with respect as the weaker partner and as
heirs with you of the gracious gift of life,
so that nothing will hinder your prayers.*
1 PETER 3:7

Lord, I know that sin hinders prayer, but I'm especially struck by the warning in today's verse that says, in essence, being inconsiderate to my wife and failing to show her proper respect will lead to a hindrance of my prayers. This shows how grievous such action is in Your eyes.

I don't express myself as well as my wife does, and sometimes that leads to me being short with her. But often, pride leads me to be short with her. Strip away my pride, Lord. My wife is the bedrock of this family. She's the love of my life. And I adore her.

THINK ABOUT IT:

Why would being inconsiderate and disrespectful toward your wife lead to a hindrance of your prayers?

DECLARING YOUR NAME

I will declare your name to my people; in the assembly I will praise you. You who fear the LORD, praise him! All you descendants of Jacob, honor him! Revere him, all you descendants of Israel!
PSALM 22:22–23

I want to be like David—leading my family into the assembly to praise You. Fellow saints gather on Sunday to do so, and too often husbands are either AWOL or coerced into going. This family will be different. I will declare Your name to my family during the week, and once we gather with other saints, I will praise Your name for all to hear. My children will never be able to say, "We didn't attend church regularly when I was growing up, so I don't see any use for it, or God, now."

THINK ABOUT IT:

What is your attitude about gathering with other saints on Sunday? Are you reluctant or joyful? What message does this send to your children?

MARRIAGE IS HONORABLE

*Marriage is honourable in all, and
the bed undefiled: but whoremongers
and adulterers God will judge.*
HEBREWS 13:4 KJV

Father, we live in an age in which marriage is
no longer honorable. In fact, it is often mocked
or considered an antiquated tradition. Sexual
debauchery of all sorts is the new normal. And
if a believer dares to say a word otherwise, he
may lose his job, his standing in the community,
and more.

Yet Your Word remains constant in saying
marriage is honorable and the marriage bed is
to remain undefiled. Regardless of what is going
on in the culture around us, strengthen my relationship with my wife on a daily basis while I
remain committed to keeping our marriage bed
undefiled.

THINK ABOUT IT:

As the culture becomes louder in its mockery
of Christians who embrace the biblical model
of marriage, what are you doing to solidify your
own marriage to make sure it doesn't crumble?

THE RIGHT PATH

Show me the right path, O LORD; point out the road for me to follow. Lead me by your truth and teach me, for you are the God who saves me. All day long I put my hope in you.
PSALM 25:4–5 NLT

Lord, I don't always know which road to take when it comes to leading and guiding my family, but I'm also not as quick as I ought to be to ask You to show me the right path. Forgive me for that. Lead me by Your truth and teach me, Father, for You are the God who saves me. I want to be able to pray along with David, who said, "All day long I put my hope in you."

THINK ABOUT IT:

Practically speaking, what would it take for you to put your hope in God all day long? Listening to Christian radio during the day? Referring to the scriptures throughout the day? Something else?

CLEANSED WITH THE WORD

Husbands, love your wives, just as Christ also loved the church and gave Himself up for her, so that He might sanctify her, having cleansed her by the washing of water with the word, that He might present to Himself the church in all her glory, having no spot or wrinkle or any such thing; but that she would be holy and blameless.
EPHESIANS 5:25–27 NASB

Loving my wife as You loved the Church, Lord, is a high calling. Just as You sanctify the sinner so we will be presentable in all our glory, You call me to wash my wife in the water of the Word. That can only happen as I devour it and plant it deeply in my own heart. May I be the type of husband who takes the initiative to read the Word to my wife, to pray it for her and over her, and to obey it.

THINK ABOUT IT:

How do you wash your wife in the water of the Word?

THE PATH OF PURITY

How can a young person stay on the path of purity? By living according to your word.
PSALM 119:9

While the writer of this psalm focuses on young people, understandably, I know this wisdom applies to everyone. Staying on the path of purity doesn't happen naturally. It requires a continual feast on Your Word, Lord. But sometimes I let the concerns of this world take priority. Rather than checking the news on my phone during my lunch hour, I could spend fifteen minutes in Your Word. Rather than spending so much time on social media during my free time, I could be working my way through a systematic study of the scriptures. If purity is what I want, then I'll seek that path according to Your Word.

THINK ABOUT IT:

If you were to record blocks of free time throughout the week, what would it say about your commitment to the Word and, ultimately, your desire to be pure?

LOVE YOUR ENEMIES

"But I say to you who hear: Love your enemies, do good to those who hate you, bless those who curse you, and pray for those who spitefully use you."
LUKE 6:27–28 NKJV

Father, my natural instinct is to protect myself and my family when we encounter enemies by either standing up to them or pulling away into a place of safety. But Your Word tells me to go against my natural instinct. If I have a neighbor who laughs at my family for attending church, You tell me to do good to them. Show me opportunities, Lord, and I'll show that person Your love. If an acquaintance curses my family, we will ask You to bless that person. And if we are used spitefully, we will pray for the offender. For what value is our faith if we aren't willing to reach out to scoffers in love?

THINK ABOUT IT:

How did you handle the situation the last time someone mocked your faith, or cursed you, or used you?

A TEACHABLE SPIRIT

*Then David said to Abigail: "Blessed is the
Lord God of Israel, who sent you this day
to meet me! And blessed is your advice and
blessed are you, because you have kept me
this day from coming to bloodshed and
from avenging myself with my own hand."*
1 Samuel 25:32–33 nkjv

Lord, when Abigail confronted David and made
him realize that killing her husband, Nabal, would
be a dire mistake, David showed a teachable
spirit. One that, when confronted with the truth,
responded immediately. May I be as teachable, Lord.

Pride is often waiting around the corner for
me, and even when I hear truth, I'm not always
as quick to respond as David. Admitting a wrong
is difficult. But holding on to it is foolish. May I
see all correction as coming from Your hand and
respond accordingly.

THINK ABOUT IT:

How do you typically respond to correction? Is
your first response defensiveness? Or do you
contemplate what is being said first?

KEEPING THE SHEEP

*And Samuel said to Jesse, "Are all the young
men here?" Then he said, "There remains yet the
youngest, and there he is, keeping the sheep."*
1 SAMUEL 16:11 NKJV

As Samuel was searching for Saul's successor
among Jesse's lineage, he examined seven of
Jesse's sons (v. 10) before asking Jesse the question in today's verse. Apparently, David was so
inconsequential as the youngest and as a keeper
of sheep that even his own father didn't consider
him for the job.

Keeping sheep was one of the most menial
jobs in the scriptures. But Bible commentator
John Gill makes this observation: "Some of the
greatest of men have been taken from rustic
employment, as Moses, Gideon, Saul, and others."

When I'm tempted to think of my own
employment as meaningless or rustic, remind
me of this fact, Father. And keep me faithful to
the tasks You've assigned me.

THINK ABOUT IT:

Do you believe your job is too menial to mean
anything? What can you learn from David?

GOD'S MASTERPIECE

*For we are God's masterpiece. He has created
us anew in Christ Jesus, so we can do the
good things he planned for us long ago.*
EPHESIANS 2:10 NLT

Father, as my children face internal or external
challenges regarding their sense of worth, may I
be quick to remind them that, in Christ, they are
Your masterpiece. You created them anew to do
good works that You planned long ago.

Help me to remind them that they don't live
in a world of random chaos, no matter how much
it might appear to be the case. Instead, You are
busy redeeming lost souls and then putting us to
work for Your kingdom and for Your glory. May
that give them a sense of peace and purpose.

THINK ABOUT IT:

How might today's verse equip you to change
your children's perspectives when they are struggling with their sense of worth?

THE SACRIFICE THAT PLEASES GOD

*And do not neglect doing good and sharing,
for with such sacrifices God is pleased.*
HEBREWS 13:16 NASB

My family has so many possessions that we don't use and will probably never pick up again. We have extra Bibles, electronic gadgets, clothing, books, toys, food, and appliances that could be put to better use elsewhere. Open our eyes to people who are lacking such items, and help us distribute them via private donations, thrift stores, collection bins, or our church. My family never wants to be one that holds on to possessions too tightly. We know that they don't belong to us anyway; they belong to You. And offering them to others is pleasing to You.

THINK ABOUT IT:

What are some practical ways you could share your possessions with people who need them? Brainstorm with your family tonight to find discreet ways to give.

DO NOT REMEMBER

Do not remember the sins of my youth or my transgressions; according to Your lovingkindness remember me, for Your goodness' sake, O Lord.
PSALM 25:7 NASB

I made so many mistakes and committed so many foolish sins in my youth, Father. In Your loving-kindness, please do not remember them. And do not revisit them in the lives of my children. I don't want them to experience the same heartache and disillusionment I experienced when I was young. Give me the wisdom to know when to talk to them about my poor choices as a youth, and give them open ears to learn from my mistakes.

THINK ABOUT IT:

Do you often fear that your children will find out about your youthful indiscretions and then use them against you to justify their own sinful behavior? Ask God for wisdom to know when to approach them for teachable moments.

TELL YOUR SONS

Tell your sons about it, and let your sons tell their sons, and their sons the next generation.
JOEL 1:3 NASB

When God sent a great famine and four types of locusts to destroy the land, He wanted Joel to make a record of the events so the old men could tell their sons, and their sons could tell their sons, all the way to the following generation.

Father, just as You are faithful to bring the blessings of Your covenant from one generation to the next, You are also faithful to bring hardship from one generation to the next in an attempt to get us to repent.

May we never curse You for hardship, but rather examine ourselves—as a family and as a country—to see if we need to repent. And if we find anything, may we be swift to do so.

THINK ABOUT IT:

What is your understanding of God's covenant? Have you considered that family hardship could be associated with sin?

THAT NONE SHALL PERISH

*The Lord is not slack concerning His promise,
as some count slackness, but is longsuffering
toward us, not willing that any should perish
but that all should come to repentance.*
2 PETER 3:9 NKJV

Lord, I pray that all my children would come to faith in Christ at a very young age; but I also know You to be a patient God, not willing that any should perish, so I ask for Your mercy and grace on my children as they contemplate making their faith their own—even if their spiritual blinders are lifted later. I'll never stop praying for their salvation, just as I know You'll never stop pursuing them. Thank You for that, Father.

THINK ABOUT IT:

Are you praying for the salvation of every unsaved family member by name? Even if they are unresponsive, take heart. God will continue to pursue them.

LIVING WITH THE LORD

*The one thing I ask of the LORD—the thing I
seek most—is to live in the house of the LORD
all the days of my life, delighting in the LORD's
perfections and meditating in his Temple.*
PSALM 27:4 NLT

Lord, I confess to thinking more about my temporal home on this earth than I do about heaven. But as I get older, I'm thinking more and more about my eternal house with You—about walking the streets of gold and worshipping the Lord Jesus Christ with all the saints for eternity.

May my children be spiritual arrows shot into the targets You've planned for them as they grow up, while also knowing that this world is not their home. What they do here matters, but it will never fully satisfy them. May they find satisfaction in knowing they will spend eternity with You.

THINK ABOUT IT:

Do you spend more time thinking about this life or the next one? How does that shape your attitude?

THE GOD OF RELATIONSHIP

"For your Father knows the things you have need of before you ask Him."
MATTHEW 6:8 NKJV

Father, I join with Bible commentator Adam Clarke in saying, "Prayer is not designed to inform God, but to give man a sight of his misery; to humble his heart, to excite his desire, to inflame his faith, to animate his hope, to raise his soul from earth to heaven, and to put him in mind that there is his Father, his country, and inheritance."

You know everything we need before we ask, but yet You want us to ask because You want that relationship with us. May I, as a husband and father, never become lax in my relationship with You. May my children see and hear me communicating with You regularly. And may they follow suit.

THINK ABOUT IT:

What's the first thought that crosses your mind when you realize that God knows your every need before you ask? How does that bolster your faith?

HAVE MERCY ON ME

Have mercy on me, LORD, for I am in distress. Tears blur my eyes. My body and soul are withering away. I am dying from grief; my years are shortened by sadness. Sin has drained my strength; I am wasting away from within.
PSALM 31:9–10 NLT

Father, I can so identify with David's prayer in Psalm 31. My seasons of sin throw me into distress, and I can feel the physical effects on my body. It drains my strength and weighs down my heart. Will I ever be free of this wretched body? My spirit yearns for holiness, but my flesh cries out for satisfaction.

Thank You, Lord Jesus, for conquering sin and death for me, because I'm incapable. Thank You for redeeming me and filling me with hope. May I model such hope to my family, in spite of my many flaws.

THINK ABOUT IT:

After a season of sin, what's your typical response? Are you able to see the bigger picture—that Christ died for your sin?

TAUGHT BY THE LORD

*"All your children shall be taught by the Lord,
and great shall be the peace of your children."*
ISAIAH 54:13 NKJV

Father, what a marvelous promise this is. The children who grow up under the protection of Your Church will learn how to live out their faith from varying perspectives and, of course, through the witness of the Holy Spirit, who resides within them. You'll see to that.

This removes a tremendous burden from me—one in which I admit to sometimes feeling as if my wife and I were solely responsible for raising our children in the faith. But You, oh Lord, will be faithful to teach them in so many other ways while my wife and I provide the best framework possible.

THINK ABOUT IT:

When you realize that God will teach your children in one way or another, how does that change your perspective?

IMITATE CHRIST

And you should imitate me,
just as I imitate Christ.
1 CORINTHIANS 11:1 NLT

The apostle Paul was the first to admit that his walk with You didn't always look the way he wanted it to. A quick reading of Romans 7:15–20 makes that clear. But he was on a continual quest to put off the old self.

In today's verse, Paul tells the Corinthian church to imitate him. Bible commentator Albert Barnes points out that this thought is a continuation from the previous chapter. "As I deny myself; as I seek to give no offence to anyone; as I endeavor not to alarm the prejudices of others, but in all things to seek their salvation, so do you," Barnes writes.

Father, may I live in such a fashion that I can say to my children, "Imitate me, just as I imitate Christ."

THINK ABOUT IT:

When you consider imitating Christ, what does that look like in your life?

THE LORD IS CLOSE

The LORD hears his people when they call to him for help. He rescues them from all their troubles. The LORD is close to the brokenhearted; he rescues those whose spirits are crushed.
PSALM 34:17–18 NLT

Lord, I want my children to understand that You hear their cry—that You are a personal God who rescues us and is close to the brokenhearted. You are there even when everybody else fails us. Even when we want to hide to nurse our wounds, You are near to us.

Psalm 139:7 (NLT) says, "I can never escape from your Spirit! I can never get away from your presence!" And verses 11–12 (NLT) say, "I could ask the darkness to hide me and the light around me to become night—but even in darkness I cannot hide from you."

THINK ABOUT IT:

Do you run toward or away from God during times of affliction or sin?

SLOW TO ANGER

But everyone must be quick to hear, slow to speak and slow to anger; for the anger of man does not achieve the righteousness of God.
JAMES 1:19–20 NASB

Father, Your Word is clear regarding anger—it does not produce the righteousness of God—but yet I am often slow to hear and quick to speak and exhibit anger. I don't always show it outwardly, but internally it is present.

Angry thoughts lead to defensiveness and incorrect conclusions. I know this. But I'm not always quick to bring my emotions under the control of the Holy Spirit. Forgive me for this, Father. Especially if my anger has provoked any fear in my wife or children. Give me a softer, kinder spirit—one that represents You to my family.

THINK ABOUT IT:

If someone were to ask your wife or children if you are an angry person, or whether you are quick to exhibit anger in your home, how would they respond?

FEEDING THE SPIRIT

For those who are according to the
flesh set their minds on the things of the
flesh, but those who are according to
the Spirit, the things of the Spirit.
ROMANS 8:5 NASB

When Paul was imprisoned in Rome, he asked for three things when Timothy visited him: "Bring the cloak which I left at Troas with Carpus, and the books, especially the parchments" (2 Timothy 4:13 NASB).

Even in prison, Paul wanted to keep his mind set on the things of the Spirit, and the best way for him to do that was to read the scriptures.

How much more should I be engaged in a similar practice? I need to spend portions of each day reading material that will feed and encourage my spirit, rather than engaging in activities that will feed my flesh. Help me do that, Father.

THINK ABOUT IT:

What are you currently reading to feed your spirit? Are you reading often enough to overcome the flesh?

THE PROMISE IS UNTO YOU

For the promise is unto you, and to your children, and to all that are afar off, even as many as the LORD our God shall call.
ACTS 2:39 KJV

Peter's sermon at Pentecost promised that You, God, would pour out Your Spirit on those who repent and are baptized (Acts 2:17, 38). And that promise is for those who were in attendance, along with their children, and those who had been dispersed, as well as others in the ages to come.

We live in the ages to come, Father. And I'm so grateful to know that You are a covenant-keeping God, one who is faithful to one generation after the next—all the way through from my children to their children. May Your Spirit always lead and guide them in the paths You've laid out for them.

THINK ABOUT IT:

When you think about God's promise in today's verse, how does it bring you comfort and joy regarding the generations behind you?

THE GOD OF SLEEP

In vain you rise early and stay up late, toiling for food to eat—for he grants sleep to those he loves.
PSALM 127:2

Father, I confess to struggling to find a work-life balance. I know a strong work ethic is important, both in practice and to model, but I also know that getting up early and staying up late for work purposes is vain—especially when I try to provide in my own strength.

Your Word says You grant sleep to those You love. May I trust You to provide for my family's needs through my strong efforts without neglecting rest. The last thing I want my grown children to say is "I wish you had been home more when we were young."

THINK ABOUT IT:

What does your current work-life balance look like? Would your family agree? Is it time to make an adjustment or two?

PRAYING FOR LEADERS

First of all, then, I urge that entreaties and prayers, petitions and thanksgivings, be made on behalf of all men, for kings and all who are in authority, so that we may lead a tranquil and quiet life in all godliness and dignity.
1 TIMOTHY 2:1–2 NASB

Father, I lift up all of our nation's leaders right now, asking for Your protection and wisdom so that my family can lead a tranquil and quiet life in all godliness and dignity. Enlighten the unenlightened, and guide the redeemed. Give them clarity where only confusion reigned previously. And bless their families with good health as well as protection from the limelight. Thank You for providing leaders at all levels, Father, for without them, we would live in chaos.

THINK ABOUT IT:

Do you pray for your leaders (at all levels) by name? If not, consider making a list of national, state, and community leaders today and begin praying for them with your family.

COMMIT TO THE LORD

*All a person's ways seem pure to them,
but motives are weighed by the LORD.
Commit to the LORD whatever you do,
and he will establish your plans.*
PROVERBS 16:2–3

Lord, I confess that I usually establish my plans and then commit them to You, rather than the other way around. But I know my motives are tainted. Remind me to commit my work, my leisure, and my family plans to You first, Father, and then leave the results to You. For You already know the future and the plans You have for us. We are willing subjects, Lord. We want what You want. May I pray accordingly during family prayer time. Lead and guide us.

THINK ABOUT IT:

Consider your most recent major decision. Did you devise a plan and then ask the Lord to bless or establish it? How might you handle similar situations in the future?

BUILDING A PROPER HOUSE

By wisdom a house is built, and through understanding it is established; through knowledge its rooms are filled with rare and beautiful treasures.
PROVERBS 24:3–4

Father, when parents build a home in wisdom, through understanding and knowledge, then its rooms are filled with rare and beautiful memories and treasures. Such wisdom, understanding, and knowledge only come through You. As we respect, encourage, pray for, and forgive one another, and keep a home—one that isn't focused on the accumulation of things—then all these things shall come to pass.

In John Gill's commentary, he says the promised beautiful treasures include "precious promises, pleasant doctrines, the valuable truths of the Gospel, and blessings of grace." May such treasures fill our home.

THINK ABOUT IT:

What is the focus of your home? Is it one another? Or is your home merely a place where you lay your head at night in preparation for the next day?

LAMPSTAND CHRISTIANS

"You are the light of the world. A city that is set on a hill cannot be hidden. Nor do they light a lamp and put it under a basket, but on a lampstand, and it gives light to all who are in the house. Let your light so shine before men, that they may see your good works and glorify your Father in heaven."
MATTHEW 5:14–16 NKJV

Jesus said that we are the light of the world and that we are to let our light so shine before men that they see our good works and glorify You, Father. This is the longing of my heart for my family. When our neighbors offend us, may we be quick to forgive them. When our community needs volunteers or leaders, may we be the first to raise our hands. Keep us engaged with others, Lord, shining for Jesus and representing Him to a lost and dying world.

THINK ABOUT IT:

In what ways could your family be considered lampstand Christians?

A HAPPY MARRIAGE

Live happily with the woman you love through all the meaningless days of life that God has given you under the sun. The wife God gives you is your reward for all your earthly toil.
ECCLESIASTES 9:9 NLT

Father, the wife You have provided for me is indeed a reward. She makes my home a humming place of activity—one my children will always remember as a place of good food, many laughs, and lots of love.

She has seen me through my most difficult of circumstances and believed in me when I didn't believe in myself. She knows my moods and my needs and is quick to accommodate them. May I always do the same for her. May she feel fulfilled in our marriage in every way possible as we grow old together.

THINK ABOUT IT:

What would your life look like without the wife God provided for you? Thank Him for doing so.

GROWING THE KINGDOM

*Take ye wives, and beget sons and daughters;
and take wives for your sons, and give your
daughters to husbands, that they may
bear sons and daughters; that ye may be
increased there, and not diminished.*
JEREMIAH 29:6 KJV

Father, even though we live in a culture that
doesn't value the traditional family as much anymore, Your thoughts have never changed. Even
when Israel had been taken into Babylonian cap-
tivity for seventy years (Jeremiah 29:10), Your
mandate for them was to get married, to have
children, and then to give away their children in
marriage so they could bear more children for
Your glory. That hasn't changed, except for those
whom You've called to a life of celibacy. Help me
to guide my children in finding spouses who also
want to see You glorified.

THINK ABOUT IT:
What type of feedback are you giving your children about their dating life? If they are too young
to date, begin considering what you'll tell them.

SIFTED LIKE WHEAT

"Simon, Simon, behold, Satan has demanded permission to sift you like wheat; but I have prayed for you, that your faith may not fail; and you, when once you have turned again, strengthen your brothers."
LUKE 22:31–32 NASB

Father, I know that as I seek to lead my family and live for You, Satan may very well demand permission to sift me like wheat, as was the case in today's passage with Peter. And if You grant him permission, then I know that just as Jesus prayed for Peter, He will pray for me.

"If they were left to themselves, they would fail; but they are kept by the power of God and the prayer of Christ," says Matthew Henry in his commentary.

I believe that, Lord. Keep me in Your grip, and deliver me safely on the other side.

THINK ABOUT IT:

Do you believe that Jesus will pray for you by name when you are being sifted? How might that change your perspective?

GUARDIAN ANGELS

*For he will command his angels concerning
you to guard you in all your ways; they will
lift you up in their hands, so that you will
not strike your foot against a stone.*
PSALM 91:11–12

Father, Your Word says that those who dwell in
the shadow of the Most High can expect certain
heavenly privileges here on earth (Psalm 91:1),
some of which include You issuing commands to
angels to guard us in all our ways.

Thank You for loving us so much to offer
such protection against Satan. Thank You for
not leaving us alone to fend for ourselves. May
I convey this message of heavenly protection
articulately to my children so they always know
that You are on their side and fighting for them.

THINK ABOUT IT:

What have you told your children about heavenly
protection? Do they know they have protection
from on high?

FAITH COMES BY HEARING

So then faith comes by hearing,
and hearing by the word of God.
ROMANS 10:17 NKJV

In Romans 10:14–15 (NKJV), Paul asks: "How then shall they call on Him in whom they have not believed? And how shall they believe in Him of whom they have not heard? And how shall they hear without a preacher? And how shall they preach unless they are sent?"

We find his conclusion in today's verse—new converts are made by hearing the Word of God. That means the Word needs to be essential in our household, Lord. It means I need to know it so well that I can teach it and share it with my children, bringing it to bear in all circumstances and, after their conversions, continuing to whet their appetites so they can do the same in the future.

THINK ABOUT IT:

How often does your family hear you read or quote the Word of God? If you are a work in progress, that's okay. Keep going!

ENDURING TEMPTATION

*Blessed is the man that endureth
temptation: for when he is tried, he shall
receive the crown of life, which the Lord
hath promised to them that love him.*
JAMES 1:12 KJV

Temptation is common for everyone, including
Jesus (Matthew 4:1–11). But when temptation
comes, I am able to endure it. I know that doesn't
mean I'll live a sin-free life—because surely I'll
stumble at times—but it does mean I have the
power within me, in the form of the Holy Spirit,
to resist. And it means I won't give myself over
to sin. As I resist, I'm promised the crown of life,
which is described by commentators as eternal
happiness—a reward for walking in the Spirit.
Thank You for such power, Lord, and thank You
for such rewards.

THINK ABOUT IT:

What does enduring temptation look like for you?
How do you endure it? Do you think about the
crown of life?

GOOD DOCTRINE

*Hear, my children, the instruction of a father,
and give attention to know understanding; for I
give you good doctrine: Do not forsake my law.*
PROVERBS 4:1–2 NKJV

God, You teach Your children in the same manner that Christian fathers are to teach their children. You offer wise instruction and good doctrine in a loving manner. For wise instruction flows from good doctrine.

Train my mind, Father, in good doctrine so that I'm able to convey it to my family. Help me to reject faulty doctrine quickly and to embrace truth even quicker. Give me a deep thirst for in-depth study of Your Word and other supporting works so that when my family asks, "How should we handle this?" I will have answers from on high.

THINK ABOUT IT:

What do you think the writer of today's verses means when he refers to "good doctrine"? How can you immerse yourself in good doctrine?

ABIDE IN ME

"Abide in Me, and I in you. As the branch cannot bear fruit of itself, unless it abides in the vine, neither can you, unless you abide in Me."
JOHN 15:4 NKJV

Father, I know that for me to live the Christian life for Your glory, I need to be a branch that receives life-giving nutrients. Abiding in You means I read Your Word regularly, implement what I'm learning from it, and then leave the results to You. It means being willing, or even expecting, to endure hardship for Your name. It means loving my enemies. And it means putting others before myself. I cannot do any of these things in my own strength. But as I abide in You, they are natural extensions of Your grace.

THINK ABOUT IT:

How would your roles as both a husband and a father look different if you were more in the habit of abiding in Christ?

ONE FLESH

Therefore shall a man leave his father and his mother, and shall cleave unto his wife: and they shall be one flesh.
GENESIS 2:24 KJV

Father, the moment I became one flesh with my wife, my former priorities became secondary. My former life, my former way of thinking, my passions, my hobbies, and everything else took a back seat to the person I chose to become when I married my wife.

Now we seek to move as one. When our interests or passions vary, we will pray, compromise, consider the other person's desires, and make a decision as a unit. Of course, we won't do this perfectly; but when we disagree, give us a spirit of mercy and grace, because we genuinely want our marriage to honor You.

THINK ABOUT IT:

Other than the marriage bed, in what ways has your marriage become "one flesh"? Do you see areas that could be improved?

TRAINING A CHILD

Train up a child in the way he should go:
and when he is old, he will not depart from it.
PROVERBS 22:6 KJV

Father, training a child in the way he should go is a privilege. It means You've entrusted me with this little blessing from above.

Bible commentator Adam Clarke describes such training this way: "Show him the duties, the dangers, and the blessings of the path; give him directions how to perform the duties, how to escape the dangers, and how to secure the blessings, which all lie before him."

May I do all of the above for my children, Lord. And may I be patient, knowing I'll need to be in a continual state of education, which often includes repetition in teachable moments.

THINK ABOUT IT:

What does training up your children in the way of the Lord look like? How could you improve?

FORGIVE ONE ANOTHER

*So, as those who have been chosen of God, holy
and beloved, put on a heart of compassion,
kindness, humility, gentleness and patience;
bearing with one another, and forgiving each
other, whoever has a complaint against anyone;
just as the Lord forgave you, so also should you.*
COLOSSIANS 3:12–13 NASB

It's a generally accepted fact that siblings will
have rivalries growing up and that teens will rebel,
become moody and irritable, and want to isolate
themselves.

Yet Your Word, oh Lord, tells us that as a
family of God, we are to be compassionate, kind,
humble, gentle, and patient with one another—
and maybe above all, forgiving, since we ourselves
are forgiven. I pray this for my family.

May we be a family that genuinely loves one
another and is willing to go the extra mile in the
expression of our love.

THINK ABOUT IT:

How might your family dynamics change if you
were to pray Colossians 3:12–13 for your family
every morning?

YOUR THORN IN THE FLESH

Because of the surpassing greatness of the revelations, for this reason, to keep me from exalting myself, there was given me a thorn in the flesh, a messenger of Satan to torment me—to keep me from exalting myself!
2 Corinthians 12:7 NASB

Lord, we don't know what Paul's thorn in the flesh was, but we know it was given to keep him from exalting himself. Whatever his ailment was, it apparently kept him down in one way or another. I don't know if I have my own thorn, but I do know that as I age, I can feel the full effects of sin in my body. While I deal with aches and pains, and maybe even something worse, I'm reminded of my humanity, much like Paul. Keep me from ever being puffed up, Father. May my family see me as a wounded but faithful warrior.

THINK ABOUT IT:

Have you ever considered that a persisting physical ailment might be your own thorn in the flesh?

CAPTIVE THOUGHTS

We are destroying speculations and every lofty thing raised up against the knowledge of God, and we are taking every thought captive to the obedience of Christ, and we are ready to punish all disobedience, whenever your obedience is complete.
2 CORINTHIANS 10:5–6 NASB

Father, as Paul described the essence of his ministry to the Corinthian church, he emphasized the importance of bringing every thought captive to the obedience of Christ. He didn't let his mind stray into areas it didn't belong. Instead, he used his mind to bring down false gods and false arguments against the one true God. He could only do so by continually renewing his mind, by rejecting the old and embracing the new. May I be that type of man to my family, Lord. May I be so engrossed in Your truth that all other arguments lose their luster.

THINK ABOUT IT:

How, specifically, are you bringing every thought captive to the obedience of Christ?

BIBLICAL DISCIPLINE

Discipline your children, and they will give you peace; they will bring you the delights you desire.
PROVERBS 29:17

Lord, I know the value of being disciplined. You've done it to me when I've strayed. My parents did it to me when I deserved it. And teachers and employers have done so as well. In all cases, it put me back on the right course. Give me the wisdom to know how to discipline my children so they too can endure a little pain right now to save them much pain later. And, according to today's verse, it will improve our relationship as well as make me proud of the people they become.

THINK ABOUT IT:

Do you discipline your children as a reactionary response? Or do you discipline them with the future in mind? The former is temporary and fleeting, while the latter is biblical discipline.

FEARING THE LORD

*Whoever fears the Lord has a secure fortress,
and for their children it will be a refuge.*
PROVERBS 14:26

Father, a healthy fear of You leaves me with no fear of man or what he can do to me. As Jesus said, "But I will show you whom you should fear: Fear him who, after your body has been killed, has authority to throw you into hell" (Luke 12:5).

Having such a healthy fear of You becomes tangible as my children see it. They embrace it as truth and as their own way of life. They can run to it as a refuge when life becomes overwhelming, and You will protect and keep them. May this be true in my life and in the lives of my children, Lord.

THINK ABOUT IT:

What does fear of the Lord look like in your life? In what ways do your children see you expressing it?

ESTABLISHED IN TRUTH

Now to Him who is able to establish you according to my gospel and the preaching of Jesus Christ, according to the revelation of the mystery which has been kept secret for long ages past. . .be the glory forever. Amen.
ROMANS 16:25, 27 NASB

Father, I pray this passage for my children this morning. Establish them, root them in Your gospel for Your glory. May they never stray from it. And may they never find anything else to establish themselves in. For nothing is as glorious or as powerful. You once kept such a revelation secret, but not any longer. Now it is freely available to all. May my children grasp it at a young age, and may it shape them in all they think, say, and do.

THINK ABOUT IT:

Did you or someone you love come to faith later in life? If so, how different might your life or theirs have looked if either of you had come to faith in Christ earlier?

GOD'S UNFAILING LOVE

Surely your goodness and unfailing love
will pursue me all the days of my life, and I
will live in the house of the Lord forever.
PSALM 23:6 NLT

Lord, I've never known a love like Yours—one
that is willing to pursue me all the days of my
life. You've pursued me while I was steeped in sin.
You've pursued me while I was in despair. You've
pursued me when I was on the verge of giving up
hope. How could I do anything other than find
refuge in the house of the Lord forever? Why
would I want to?

May my children know this love, Lord. And
may they feel it even now, no matter what they
are going through. Your love is the only thing
that can truly see them through.

THINK ABOUT IT:

Is there anything your love wouldn't compel you
to do for your children, no matter what they've
done? How much more so is that true of God's
love for you?

PROCLAIMING GOD'S POWER

O God, you have taught me from my earliest childhood, and I constantly tell others about the wonderful things you do. Now that I am old and gray, do not abandon me, O God. Let me proclaim your power to this new generation, your mighty miracles to all who come after me.
PSALM 71:17–18 NLT

Lord, ever since I met You, I've been telling people about Your saving power and Your amazing love. As I age, do not abandon me, for I want to continue to proclaim Your power to my children and Your mighty miracles to each generation that comes after me as long as I have breath to do so. Use my words, my testimony, and my life however You see fit, Lord, to bring the generations in my family to You.

THINK ABOUT IT:

As you age, are you just as quick to proclaim God's power to the generations behind you as you were when you were younger? Why or why not?

PURSUE PEACE

*Pursue peace with all men, and the sanctification
without which no one will see the Lord.*
HEBREWS 12:14 NASB

Lord, You place such a high value on peace that
You sent Your Son to die that we might have
peace with You. May my actions never stir up
dissension in my sphere of influence. May I never
goad people to anger or strife. As Albert Barnes
says in his commentary, "We are to make war with
sin, but not with people; with bad passions and
corrupt desires, but not with our fellow-worms."

Of course, this can be applied to father-
children relationships. I've known fathers who
alienated their children, and peace was far
from them. May that never be the case with my
family, Lord.

THINK ABOUT IT:

Do you have a strained relationship with any of
your children right now? If so, go the extra mile
in offering reconciliation. Admit fault for your
side of the argument, and extend an olive branch.

CROWNS OF OLD MEN

Grandchildren are the crown of old men,
and the glory of sons is their fathers.
PROVERBS 17:6 NASB

Father, I know that large families were seen as blessings in the Hebrew culture and that living to see multiple generations grow up in the faith was even better. As much as we don't value large families in today's Western culture, I certainly will see my grandchildren as a crown. And I pray that my children see me as their glory.

May my children grow up honoring You and adhering to the biblical principles they were taught in their youth. And may their children follow suit so that one day, nobody in the family line can remember a time when a generation did not worship You.

THINK ABOUT IT:

What do you think today's verse means when it refers to grandchildren being a crown of old men?

THE IMMORAL WOMAN

So she [an immoral woman] seduced him with her
pretty speech and enticed him with her flattery.
He followed her at once, like an ox going to the
slaughter. He was like a stag caught in a trap,
awaiting the arrow that would pierce its heart.
PROVERBS 7:21–23 NLT

Father, the immoral woman who seduced the
man in today's verses took advantage of his care-
lessness and lack of wisdom. He went strolling
down the path by her house at twilight, and she
approached him in seductive clothing. She threw
herself at him, using seductive language, and
offered him forbidden fruit (vv. 8–20). Before he
knew it, he was caught in her trap, "little knowing
it would cost him his life" (v. 23 NLT). Help me
to avoid this woman, Lord. May I never even
approach the path by her home.

THINK ABOUT IT:

How close to this woman's path have you allowed
yourself to get?

A RESURRECTION OF LIFE

*"Do not marvel at this; for an hour is
coming, in which all who are in the tombs will
hear His voice, and will come forth; those
who did the good deeds to a resurrection
of life, those who committed the evil
deeds to a resurrection of judgment."*
JOHN 5:28–29 NASB

Father, help me convey to my children the importance of not placing too high a priority on the things of this world, while at the same time helping them understand that what they do in the here and now matters for all eternity. I know that they cannot earn their salvation, but their good deeds will follow them, as will their evil deeds if they are unconverted. Lord, save my children and grow them into pillars of the faith—people who are focused on doing good deeds, knowing You've promised them eternal life.

THINK ABOUT IT:

How do today's verses compare with what you are teaching your children about good deeds?

BEFORE HE FORMED THEM

Before I formed thee in the belly I knew thee; and before thou camest forth out of the womb I sanctified thee, and I ordained thee a prophet unto the nations.
JEREMIAH 1:5 KJV

Lord, just as You knew Jeremiah in his mother's womb and sanctified him to become a prophet to the nations, You also knew my children in my wife's womb, and I pray that You would sanctify them for Your purposes—whether full-time Christian work or otherwise.

May I always be quick to share this information with them—that You are a sanctifying God who sets His people aside for His intended purposes. And may I be quick to help my children realize what Your purposes are and then to facilitate those realizations.

THINK ABOUT IT:

How are you helping your children (no matter their ages) realize their intended purpose?

PRAYING THE BENEDICTION

The Lord bless thee, and keep thee: the Lord make his face shine upon thee, and be gracious unto thee: the Lord lift up his countenance upon thee, and give thee peace.
NUMBERS 6:24–26 KJV

Lord, just as You told Moses to tell Aaron and his sons to bless the people of Israel with the special blessings found in today's verses, I pray these blessings over my family this morning. Bless and keep my family from all harm today. Make Your face shine on all they do at school, home, or work. Be gracious to them when they stumble. Lift up Your countenance on them and give them peace, no matter their struggle or turmoil. For without Your blessings, we would surely fall.

THINK ABOUT IT:

If you incorporated this prayer for your family into your day—maybe even verbally before they left each morning—how might this set them on the right course?

BEAUTIFUL FEET

How beautiful on the mountains are the feet of the messenger who brings good news, the good news of peace and salvation, the news that the God of Israel reigns!
ISAIAH 52:7 NLT

Lord, we tend to view mountains and nature in general as beautiful, but in today's verse, You say that the feet of messengers who bring good news on mountains are beautiful. In other words, as we go into remote regions to tell others about peace and salvation through the finished work of Christ, that's true beauty.

I pray for my family's feet today. Point them toward the shunned, the disenfranchised, the abused, the neglected, the frightened, and the skeptical, and shine the light of Christ through them. Give them the right words to say at the right time. For indeed, the God of Israel reigns!

THINK ABOUT IT:

Are you hesitant to see your family take the good news to people who might not be receptive? Pray for today's verse to change your heart.

KEEP SHORT ACCOUNTS

*Then I acknowledged my sin to you and
did not cover up my iniquity. I said, "I will
confess my transgressions to the LORD."
And you forgave the guilt of my sin.*
PSALM 32:5

Lord, I know You to be a forgiving God—one who
is long-suffering and patient, but one who does
require an acknowledgment of sin. As I keep
short accounts with You, You are quick to offer
forgiveness from the guilt of my sin. May I always
be quick to turn to You rather than covering up
my iniquity. And may I always be quick to ask my
family for forgiveness when I have wronged them.
Finding forgiveness through the shed blood of
Your Son is refreshing and cause for celebration.
Thank You, Lord.

THINK ABOUT IT:

Are you currently covering up any iniquities?
Ask God to search your heart, and whatever sins
He reveals, be quick to confess them to Him so
you can approach the day with a renewed spirit.

FAMILY UNITY

"It is he [John] who will go as a forerunner before Him in the spirit and power of Elijah, TO TURN THE HEARTS OF THE FATHERS BACK TO THE CHILDREN, *and the disobedient to the attitude of the righteous, so as to make ready a people prepared for the Lord."*
LUKE 1:17 NASB

Lord, just as the Jews were divided into different sects with different beliefs when the Gospel of Luke was written, so it is with Your Church today. John went ahead of Jesus to turn the hearts of the fathers back to the children, for even families were divided, much like they are now.

Father, may theological disagreements never separate our family. May we maintain our focus on Jesus and His redeeming work, rather than our personal beliefs. And may my children always feel the freedom to ask theological questions.

THINK ABOUT IT:

As your children mature in the faith and take on their own theological beliefs, how will you handle the situation when theirs vary from yours?

RUN TOWARD THE SINNER

"So he [the prodigal son] got up and came to his father. But while he was still a long way off, his father saw him and felt compassion for him, and ran and embraced him and kissed him."
LUKE 15:20 NASB

The father in the parable of the lost son represents You, Lord—a God who is not only quick to forgive but also willing to run toward Your children when we rise out of our own pigpens and head back home. Your forgiveness isn't conditional, nor is it nominal. Instead, You embrace and kiss us upon our return.

May I be that type of father. May I never keep a record of wrongs or be reluctant to show affection upon my children's return. Yes, I know I could get burned. But I'd rather model Your love, Lord, than one that is conditional.

THINK ABOUT IT:

How does your physical and emotional countenance compare with the father in this parable when one of your children needs forgiveness?

OUR EARTHLY REWARD

Here is what I have seen to be good and fitting: to eat, to drink and enjoy oneself in all one's labor in which he toils under the sun during the few years of his life which God has given him; for this is his reward.
ECCLESIASTES 5:18 NASB

Even though life is short, You, Father, have given us so many ways to find joy here on earth. Breaking bread with my family is among the most special of times. May my wife and I always guard that time. And finding pleasure in the simple things—family walks, fishing trips, cooking, reading to one another, birthday parties, and the like—brings laughter and satisfaction. Thank You, Lord, for being the God of both heaven and earth.

THINK ABOUT IT:

How much joy do you find in the simple things of life? Are you quick to overlook them in search of something else?

TROUBLE CHASES SINNERS

Trouble chases sinners, while
blessings reward the righteous.
PROVERBS 13:21 NLT

Lord, I know from experience that one sin usually leads to the next one. And before long, it feels like sin is chasing us. The same is true for blessings. As we perform good works, Your blessings from on high follow us and we can be sure to receive our reward.

Help me to convey these truths to my children. Give me real-life examples of both. When we see real-life examples of trouble chasing sinners, may we pray for them as a family and offer our support. When we see real-life examples of blessings following the righteous, may it encourage our faith and increase our desire to do even more.

THINK ABOUT IT:

In your experience, does trouble chase sinners? How does one break that cycle? How have you broken that cycle?

FREED FROM SIN

For he who has died is freed from sin.
ROMANS 6:7 NASB

Father, we know that Satan frequently lies to us about the satisfaction of sin, but yet we often fall for it.

In his devotional *Morning and Evening*, Charles Spurgeon makes this observation about today's verse: "Did sin ever yield thee real pleasure? Didst thou find solid satisfaction in it? If so, go back to thine old drudgery, and wear the chain again, if it delight thee. But inasmuch as sin did never give thee what it promised to bestow, but deluded thee with lies, be not a second time snared by the old fowler—be free, and let the remembrance of thy ancient bondage forbid thee to enter the net again!"

May we be a family that desires to never enter the net again.

THINK ABOUT IT:

What does it mean to be free from sin? How does Christ's death empower you, and your family, to never enter the net again?

ACKNOWLEDGING GOD

*"Let us acknowledge the L*ORD*; let us press on to acknowledge him. As surely as the sun rises, he will appear; he will come to us like the winter rains, like the spring rains that water the earth."*
HOSEA 6:3

Lord, in today's verse we are told to press on to acknowledge You and that, as surely as the sun rises, You will appear. Pressing on implies effort on my part. If I am to press on to acknowledge You, then that means forgoing the wisdom of this world for Your wisdom. It means increasing in my knowledge of You. And it means following You and Your ways when the world will laugh. As I lean into You, You will appear. Oh, how I long for my children to fully grasp this principle. May it be so, Lord.

THINK ABOUT IT:

What does your family do, at your leading, that sets you apart from your neighbors? In what ways are you acknowledging God that might lead to them taking notice?

EVEN IF HE DOESN'T

"If we are thrown into the blazing furnace, the God whom we serve is able to save us. He will rescue us from your power, Your Majesty. But even if he doesn't, we want to make it clear to you, Your Majesty, that we will never serve your gods or worship the gold statue you have set up."
DANIEL 3:17–18 NLT

Shadrach, Meshach, and Abednego were young people who refused to worship the gold statue that Nebuchadnezzar set up. And they refused again when confronted by the king, even when threatened with the blazing furnace. They were willing to be burned alive, knowing You could rescue them; but even if You chose not to, they made it clear that they would never worship the gold statue.

May You grant such faith and fortitude deep into the hearts of my own children. May they bow to You only.

THINK ABOUT IT:

What are you doing right now to infuse this type of faith into your children?

USE OUR POSSESSIONS, LORD

Honor the LORD with your possessions, and with the firstfruits of all your increase; so your barns will be filled with plenty, and your vats will overflow with new wine.
PROVERBS 3:9–10 NKJV

Lord, all that my family owns is Yours to do with as You please. Use our house for hospitality. Use our vehicle to transport others to appointments, work, Bible studies, and worship. Use our extra clothing to clothe the naked. Use our abundance of food to feed the hungry. Use our library to increase people's understanding of You. Use it all, Lord, for it all belongs to You anyway. And may we always offer our firstfruits out of our increase. We know that as we do all these things, You will watch over us.

THINK ABOUT IT:

In what ways are you allowing the Lord to use your possessions? Could your family do a better job?

IN THE BEGINNING

In the beginning God created the heavens and the earth.
GENESIS 1:1 NKJV

Lord, so much hinges on the truth of the first sentence in Your holy Word. In the beginning, You created the heavens and the earth. You are the Creator. You are the Sustainer. You are the King of the earth. You own it all. You rule it all. And I praise You for that.

Help me to continually teach the truths of Genesis 1:1 to my children. When the world confronts them about evolution, may Genesis 1:1 prevail. When people mistreat the earth and justify it to them, may Genesis 1:1 prevail. When my children are tempted to become their own kings and do things their own way, may Genesis 1:1 prevail.

THINK ABOUT IT:

Have you had a discussion with your family about the many implications of Genesis 1:1?

LEAST OR GREAT?

"Whoever then annuls one of the least of these commandments, and teaches others to do the same, shall be called least in the kingdom of heaven; but whoever keeps and teaches them, he shall be called great in the kingdom of heaven."
MATTHEW 5:19 NASB

Father, the Pharisees often divided the commands of God into lesser and greater; therefore, they taught that those who violated the lesser commands were guilty of minor infractions. But in today's verse, Jesus decimates such claims, saying to annul even the least of the commandments will lead to a believer being called the least in the kingdom of heaven.

May we be a family that never views Your commands as the Pharisees did. Instead, may we go further in both keeping and teaching Your commands to anybody who will listen.

THINK ABOUT IT:

Have you ever considered that you and your family will either be called the least in the kingdom of heaven or great in the kingdom of heaven, depending on your actions?

A SYMPATHETIC HIGH PRIEST

Therefore, since we have a great high priest who has passed through the heavens, Jesus the Son of God, let us hold fast our confession. For we do not have a high priest who cannot sympathize with our weaknesses, but One who has been tempted in all things as we are, yet without sin.
HEBREWS 4:14–15 NASB

Lord, if I teach my children anything that has lasting effects, may it be a spirit of prayer during times of tribulation and temptation. For You, Jesus, can sympathize with our weaknesses, having been tempted in all things, just as we are, yet without sin. You can sustain us to hold fast to our confession when the world mocks us. And You can empower us to overcome temptation when Satan targets us.

THINK ABOUT IT:

During times of tribulation or temptation, what is your typical first reaction? Resolve to turn to Christ first going forward, and in so doing, set an example for your children that will last a lifetime.

SCRIPTURE INDEX

OLD TESTAMENT